SPECULUM ANNIVERSARY MONOGRAPHS

FOUR

The Psalter and Hours of
Yolande of Soissons

SPECULUM ANNIVERSARY MONOGRAPHS

FOUR

The Psalter and Hours of Yolande of Soissons

KAREN GOULD

THE MEDIAEVAL ACADEMY OF AMERICA   1978

*The publication of this book was made possible by funds contributed
to the Mediaeval Academy during the Semi-Centennial Fund Drive.*

Copyright © 1978. Cambridge, Massachusetts
By the Mediaeval Academy of America
LCC: 78-55888
ISBN: 910956-64-2
Printed in the United States of America

To my mother and to the memory of my father

Contents

List of Illustrations   ix

List of Tables   xi

Preface   xiii

Chapter

    I   THE MANUSCRIPT

         Origins and History   1

         The Text   13

    II   THE ILLUMINATIONS

         The Style   25

         Related Manuscripts   35

         The Amiens Style and Parisian Illumination   53

    III   ICONOGRAPHIC PROBLEMS

         The Miniature Cycles   65

         The Unicorn Parable   76

         The Holy Face   81

         The Franciscan Iconography   94

         St. Firmin and the Localization of M729   108

Appendices

    A   The Contents of M729   117

    B   Calendar   119

    C   Litany   124

    D   Suffrages   126

Index of Manuscripts   127

The illustrations are printed following page 128. Figures 1–39 are from the Psalter and Hours of Yolande of Soissons, New York, Pierpont Morgan Library, M729.

1a. Yolande of Soissons with Her Family, fol. 1v
1b. St. Francis Preaching to the Birds, fol. 2r
  2. The Invention of the Body of St. Firmin, fol. 3r
  3. Crucifixion, fol. 4v
  4. Noli me tangere, fol. 6v
  5. Calendar, fol. 10v
  6. Calendar, fol. 11r
  7. Holy Face, fol. 15r
  8. Beatus Page, fol. 16r
  9. Psalm 26: David Looking to God, fol. 40r
10. Temptation on the Mountain, fol. 55v
11. Text: Psalter, fol. 63v
12. Raising of Lazarus; Psalm 52: The Fool, fols. 70v, 71r
13. Text: Psalter, fol. 79v
14. Miracle of the Loaves, fol. 85v
15. Healing the Blind Man at the Pool of Siloam, fol. 104v
16. Woman Taken in Adultery, fol. 122v
17. Psalm 97: Priests Singing, fol. 123r
18. Litany: Priests Singing, fol. 196r
19. Yolande of Soissons Praying, fol. 232v
20. Matins of the Virgin: Annunciation, fol. 233r
21. Nativity, fol. 246v
22. Suffrages: Annunciation and Saints Peter and Paul, fol. 255v
23. Suffrages: Noli me tangere, fol. 259v
24. Prime of the Virgin: Magi before Herod, fol. 268r
25. Creation of the Plants, fol. 272v
26. Adoration of the Magi, fol. 275v
27. Nones of the Holy Spirit: Peter Healing a Lame Man, fol. 287r
28. Legend of the Cornfield, fol. 289v
29. Massacre of the Innocents, fol. 296v
30. Death of the Virgin, fol. 305v
31. Compline of the Virgin: Coronation of the Virgin, fol. 306r
32. Text: Hours of the Virgin, fol. 309r
33. Entry into Jerusalem, fol. 310v
34. Lauds of the Cross: St. John, fol. 315r
35. Crucifixion, fol. 332v

36. Crucifixion, fol. 337v
37. Tree of Life, fol. 345v
38. Unicorn Parable, fol. 354v
39. Office of the Dead: Funeral Rites, fol. 355r
40. Amiens Cathedral, Chevet
41. Amiens Cathedral, West Façade
42. Psalter of St. Louis, Paris, Bibliothèque Nationale, MS lat. 10525: Balaam and His Ass, fol. 39v
43. Missal, Amiens, Bibliothèque Municipale, MS 157: Nativity, fol. 23r
44. Missal, MS 157: Queen Bathildis, fol. 29r
45. Missal, MS 157: Crucifixion, fol. 109v
46. Missal, MS 157: Coronation of the Virgin, fol. 110r
47. Psalter, Amiens, Bibliothèque Municipale, MS 124: Calendar, November, fol. 6r
48. Psalter, MS 124: Beatus Page, fol. 17v
49. Missal, Amiens, Bibliothèque Municipale, MS 156: Nativity, fol. 21r
50. Missal, MS 156: Decorated Initial, fol. 273r
51. Psalter, New York, Pierpont Morgan Library, M796: Beatus Page, fol. 1r
52. Psalter, M796: Psalm 80, David Playing Bells; Text, fols. 75v, 76r
53. Psalter, M796: Psalm 109, God and Christ, fol. 106r
54. Psalter, Paris, Bibliothèque Nationale, MS lat. 10435: Beatus Page, fol. 1r
55. Psalter, MS lat. 10435: Psalm 119, fol. 150r
56. *Livre de Sidrach,* Paris, Bibliothèque Nationale, MS fr. 1159: Noah Directing the Animals to the Ark, fol. 59v
57. Arthurian Cycle, Bonn, Universitätsbibliothek, MS 526, fol. 1r
58. *Histoire du Graal,* Paris, Bibliothèque Nationale, MS fr. 95, fol. 1r
59. *Histoire du Graal,* MS fr. 95, fol. 205r
60. Martyrology of Saint-Germain-des-Prés, Paris, Bibliothèque Nationale, MS lat. 12834: July, fol. 59v
61. Evangeliary, London, British Library, MS Add. 17341: Entry into Jerusalem, fol. 1r
62. Evangeliary, MS Add. 17341: Genesis Initial, fol. 11r
63. Tomb of Adelaide of Champagne, Joigny, Saint-Jean
64. Matthew Paris, *Chronica Majora,* Cambridge, Corpus Christi College, MS 16: Veronica, fol. 49v
65. The Holy Face, Laon Cathedral
66. Psalter of Gérard de Damville, New York, Pierpont Morgan Library, M72: St. Francis Preaching to the Birds, fol. 139v
67. *Vergier de Solas,* Paris, Bibliothèque Nationale, MS fr. 9220: Tree of Life, fol. 9v
68. Amiens Cathedral, West Façade, Tympanum of the St. Firmin Portal

Tables

1. The Coats of Arms   2
2. Usage of the Hours of the Virgin, M729   15
3. Cycles of Illustrations   66

Of medieval illuminated manuscripts in need of scholarly attention, the Psalter and Hours of Yolande of Soissons, now in the Pierpont Morgan Library, M729, is among the most important. Dated by previous scholarship in the last quarter of the thirteenth century and localized in northern France, possibly at Amiens, the manuscript is remarkable not only for its extensive program of decoration, which leaves almost no page untouched by the illuminator's hand, but also for the consistently high quality of the painting. This richly illustrated Psalter and Hours was produced during a highly creative period in Gothic art, a period marked by important changes in the aesthetic of the illuminated manuscript. Many of the stylistic characteristics in M729, such as the convincing modeling of figures and the experimentation with spatial effects, represent significant contributions to these late-thirteenth-century stylistic developments. In addition, the fullness of illustration presents a carefully conceived iconographic scheme that visually expresses a trend in religious attitudes toward personal and individual meditation for the laity.

Despite M729's importance in the history of Gothic manuscript illumination, it has received neither adequate treatment nor full publication. The most extensive published descriptions of the Psalter and Hours of Yolande of Soissons come from exhibition catalogues.[1] These entries have described the general stylistic characteristics of the illumination, noting especially the fullness of the decoration, the bright colors, the combination of fluid line with modeled colors, and the architectural borders. The stylistic problem that has most intrigued scholars, however, is M729's relationship to the illumination associated with Master Honoré, an artist who worked in Paris at the end of the thirteenth century and

1. The New York Public Library, *Illuminated Manuscripts from the Pierpont Morgan Library* (New York, 1934), p. 25; The Pierpont Morgan Library, *The First Quarter Century of the Pierpont Morgan Library* (New York, 1949), p. 35, pl. 13; The Walters Art Gallery, *Illuminated Books of the Middle Ages and Renaissance* (Baltimore, 1949), p. 24, pl. 27; William D. Wixom, *Treasures from Medieval France* (Cleveland, 1967), pp. 168–171, 364–365; The National Gallery of Canada, *Art and the Courts: France and England from 1259 to 1328,* 2 vols. (Ottawa, 1972), 1:64, 86–87; 2:pls. 21, 22.

whose style marked a significant turning point in French Gothic illumination. The figure style displayed in the Psalter and Hours of Yolande of Soissons, particularly the assurance of the modeling, has been said to "announce the style of Master Honoré," without being included as part of the manuscripts thought to represent Honoré's work.[2] Also, some of the iconographic problems connected with the Yolande Psalter and Hours have received brief notices, but the integration of these themes into the manuscript's entire program of decoration has not been examined.[3]

2. Erwin Panofsky, *Early Netherlandish Painting* (Cambridge, Mass., 1953), p. 15 n.3. The Walters Art Gallery catalogue, *Illuminated Books*, p. 24, also mentions that the most skillful artist of M729 worked in "a style resembling that ascribed to 'Maître Honoré' of Paris." Gerhard Schmidt, discussing the origins of Honoré's style in *Die Malerschule von St. Florian: Beiträge zur süddeutschen Malerei zu Ende des 13. und im 14. Jahrhundert* (Linz, 1962), p. 115, notes that Panofsky and the Walters Art Gallery catalogue had suggested that the style of M729 could have been a forerunner of Master Honoré's painting. Larry Ayres, "The Miniatures of the Santa Barbara Bible: A Preliminary Report," *Soundings: Collections of the University Library* [University of California at Santa Barbara] 3 (1971), 7–8, notes that some art historians have found precedents for Honoré's style in M729, but he also considers the possibility that the stylistic resemblances represent parallel developments. D. H. Turner, "The Development of Maître Honoré," *The Eric George Millar Bequest of Manuscripts and Drawings, 1967* (London, 1968), p. 57, also says that the style of one of the M729 artists was "particularly close to Honoré," but he thinks that the date of M729 is probably later than 1275 and that stylistically "the illumination in the manuscript M729 which closest resembles Honoré's will be seen to have that unoriginal closeness which implies dependence or derivation." For a review of some of the literature relating to stylistic questions concerning M729 see the articles by Ellen J. Beer, "Gotische Buchmalerei. Literatur von 1945 bis 1961, Forsetzung," *Zeitschrift für Kunstgeschichte* 27 (1964), 166, and "Gotische Buchmalerei. Literatur von 1962 bis 1965 mit Nachträgen für die Jahre 1957 bis 1961," *Zeitschrift für Kunstgeschichte* 30 (1967), 85. For the place of M729 in connection with broader questions about northern French illumination see M. Alison Stones, "The Illustration of the French Prose 'Lancelot' in Flanders, Belgium and Paris: 1250–1340," Ph.D. Dissertation (University of London, 1970), pp. 179–180.

3. Millard Meiss, *Painting in Florence and Siena after the Black Death* (Princeton, 1951), p. 148, fig. 157, cites the miniature of the Nativity in M729 as an example of possible northern European influence on the iconography of Italian Nativity scenes. Panofsky, *Early Netherlandish Painting*, pp. 127 n.5, 278 n.1., calls attention to the midwife preparing the bath and the animals biting the bedclothes in the crib in the M729 Nativity. Panofsky also discusses the foot-kissing motif in the Adoration of the Magi (p. 23 n.2) and the meaning of the *Lignum vitae* Crucifixion (p. 140). Panofsky in "The Mouse that Michelangelo Failed to Carve," *Essays in Memory of Karl Lehmann*, Marsyas Supplement 1 (New York, 1964), p. 244 n.8, identifies the textual source for the small animals gnawing the tree in the illustration of the Unicorn Parable. Hans Wentzel, "Die Kornfeldlegende in Parchim, Lübeck, den Niederlanden, England, Frankreich und Skandinavien," *Festschrift*

Numerous problems concerning the Psalter and Hours of Yolande of Soissons remain unresolved. The first and major question involves a more precise localization and dating of the manuscript. With a firmer resolution of this central issue, it is possible to inquire a step further into the role that M729 played in late-thirteenth-century illumination. Of special importance is its relationship to northern French and Parisian manuscript decoration. There are additional problems concerning the sources for the selection and depiction of many of the iconographic themes.

This study attempts to answer some of these questions by utilizing the wide range of possibilities that the manuscript offers for analysis. First, an examination of the manuscript as a whole explores various types of evidence. The systematic use of heraldic devices helps to identify the person for whom M729 was made and to place it in an historical context. Parts of the text such as the saints of particular veneration in the calendar and the dialect of the sections in Old French provide other clues for localization. A second approach focuses on the style of the illustrations. This study not only describes and analyzes the basic stylistic features of M729 but also places this Psalter and Hours in a broader perspective by pointing to similar stylistic elements in other manuscripts. Finally, a consideration of the iconography of M729's illuminations adds further support for M729's place of production and demonstrates the importance of this manuscript in developing a visual expression for the new religious approaches of the late Middle Ages. The combined evaluation of this evidence gives a clearer understanding of the place of the Psalter and Hours of Yolande of Soissons in French art and culture of the Gothic period.

It is a pleasure to acknowledge the assistance and cooperation I received during the course of my research. The staffs of the Pierpont Morgan Library, the Bibliothèque Municipale of Amiens, the Bibliothèque Nationale and the Bibliothèque de l'Arsenal in Paris, the British Library, the Bodleian Library, the Beinicke Library at Yale University, the Walters Art Gallery, and the Humanities Research Center at the University of Texas at Austin were unfailingly helpful. I owe special thanks to the Interlibrary

Kurt Bauch (Munich, 1957), p. 184, discusses the Legend of the Cornfield miniature. Lilian Randall, *Images in the Margins of Gothic Manuscripts* (Berkeley, 1966), pp. 34, 66, 69, 72, 92, 95, 102, 106, 110, 121, 122, 124, 140, 146, 155, 166, 178, 198, 213, 235, fig. 383, provides references to themes in the marginal illustrations, and Wixom, *Treasures from Medieval France*, p. 170, gives an interpretation of the Beatus page marginalia. Gertrud Schiller, *Iconography of Christian Art*, trans. Janet Seligman, (Greenwich, Conn., 1968), p. 111, mentions the Magi kissing the Christ Child's foot in the Adoration of the Magi.

Loan Service at the Perry-Castañeda Library at the University of Texas at Austin.

The Pierpont Morgan Library, the Bibliothèque Nationale, the Bibliothèque Municipale at Amiens, the Universitätsbibliothek at Bonn, the British Library Board, and the Master and Fellows of Corpus Christi College, Cambridge, graciously granted permission to reproduce photographs of manuscripts in their collections. I owe thanks for other pictures to James Austin of Cambridge, England, and Hirmer Fotoarchiv München.

Several librarians and curators provided valuable information and guidance, and I am grateful to François Avril, Janet Backhouse, Lilian Randall, William Voelkle, and the late Dorothy Miner. For aid with research and interpretation, provided through correspondence and conversation, I would like to thank Larry Ayres, Carl Barnes, Leonard Boyle, Gerard J. Brault, Willene Clark, William W. Clark, Ruth J. Dean, Doug Farquhar, Richard Rouse, Eleanor Spencer, Alison Stones, Rosalie Vermette, Linda Voigts, and the late Robert Branner.

William Kibler and Janet Meisel improved the manuscript with their critical readings. Eleanor Greenhill introduced me to the subject of manuscript illumination, suggested this topic, and encouraged me throughout the preparation of this monograph. I am most appreciative of her constant willingness to share with me the results of her wide-ranging scholarship and to devote so much energy to my work.

My husband, Lewis L. Gould, withstood the years of research and writing with patience and good humor. His incisive comments improved this study.

The dedication is a small expression of thanks to my mother and father, Helen and John L. Keel, for their constant support.

Any errors of fact or interpretation are my sole responsibility.

THE MANUSCRIPT

ORIGINS AND HISTORY

The Psalter and Hours of Yolande of Soissons, in its present state, is a manuscript of 437 numbered folios that measures 137 by 179 millimeters.[1] The parchment, of uniformly good quality, is ruled in a consistent pattern with a text space of nineteen lines measuring 78 by 107 millimeters.[2] The script is a Gothic *textualis formata* written in incaustum. Both French and Latin rubrics are used. As a look at this manuscript's history will indicate, M729's composition has been disrupted on several occasions, and the present arrangement is a result of its most recent rebinding, in blue leather, blind tooled and stamped, done by Duprez Lahey in 1927 after it came to the Pierpont Morgan Library.[3] The extensive decorative program, one of this manuscript's most outstanding features, consists of thirty-nine full-page miniatures, sixty-four historiated initials, small calendar miniatures, numerous full-page and partial borders, as well as small decorated initials.

The coats of arms that form an integral part of the border decoration point to the identity of M729's first owner. Each of the borders accompanying miniatures and historiated initials has at least four roundels filled with shields that bear heraldic devices (figs. 1, 5, 9). Only six different heraldic devices, however, are repeated on the approximately 400 shields.[4]

1. Folios 435–437 are paper flyleaves at the back. There are three flyleaves numbered i, ii, iii at the front. The collation is: 7 single leaves, 1^6, 2 single leaves, $2^8(-1)$, $3-27^8$, $28^8(-1,2)$, $29-53^8$, $54^8(-8)$.
2. The rulings of the text pages are 18.[6.72] .6.17.6.2 mm. × 19.[6.46.5.44.6] .26.6. 21 mm. The brackets indicate the text space. The measurements vary slightly from folio to folio. Within the text space, the two lines marking the top, middle (tenth line of writing), and bottom lines extend to the edge of the right margin, but usually not into the left margin. Prickings are visible at times at the top and the bottom of the page, but the prickings on the side appear to have been trimmed. The average height of each line of writing is between 5 and 6 mm. Only the calendar rulings differ. They are: 18.[9.6.9.6.71].14 mm. × 19.[135].26 mm., also varying slightly from page to page.
3. The binder's name is stamped on the front pastedown.
4. For a chart recording the distribution of the coats of arms see Karen Gould, "The Psalter and Hours of Yolande of Soissons," Ph.D. Dissertation (University of Texas

Table 1: THE COATS OF ARMS

Contemporary French and English sources provide the identification for four of the six coats of arms. The heraldic device of *azure, semy of lis or with a demi-lion argent over all* (Table 1a, fig. 1), belonged to the Moreuil family, and the counts of Soissons bore *or, a lion passant gules*

with a border of the same (Table 1f, fig. 19).[5] The Hangest family coat of arms was *argent, a cross gules charged with five scallops or* (Table 1c, fig. 4), while the device of *barruly or and gules* (Table 1d, fig. 1) was connected with the counts of Grandpré.[6]

Although the two remaining coats of arms cannot be so readily identified the heraldic combination of Moreuil, Soissons, Hangest, and Grandpré makes Yolande of Soissons the most likely original owner of M729. The wife of Bernard V of Moreuil, she was the daughter of Raoul of Soissons and his wife, Comtesse of Hangest.[7] The third wife of her paternal grandfather, Raoul I, count of Soissons, was Ade of Grandpré, who was possibly Yolande's grandmother.[8]

at Austin, 1975), pp. 346–357. Although the heraldic shields are not placed in any particular order or pattern throughout the manuscript, the two devices belonging to Bernard of Moreuil and Yolande of Soissons appear more frequently than the other four, and these two coats of arms are the only two devices used in the Psalter section (excluding the litany). The Soissons device is the only coat of arms that is not used before the Book of Hours section. It first appears on fol. 228v at Lauds of the Holy Spirit.

5. The Moreuil blazon is recorded in the Chifflet-Prinet armorial, a copy that Jules Chifflet made of an armorial probably compiled in 1297 by a herald with Robert II, count of Artois. Max Prinet, "Armorial de France composé à la fin du 13e siècle ou au commencement du 14e," *Le Moyen Age* 31 (1920), 23, No. 53; Paul Adam-Even, "Rôle d'armes de l'ost de Flandres (juin 1297)," *Archivum Heraldicum* 78 (1959), 2–7; Gerard J. Brault, *Eight Thirteenth Century Rolls of Arms in French and Anglo-Norman Blazon* (University Park, Penn., 1973), p. 79, No. 53. For identification of the Soissons coat of arms see Paul Adam-Even and Léon Jéquier, "Un Armorial français du 13e siècle. L'Armorial Wijnbergen," *Archives Héraldiques Suisses* 68 (1954), 58, No. 827; Brault, *Eight Thirteenth Century Rolls of Arms*, p. 47, No. 38; p. 71, No. 91.

6. For the Hangest coat of arms see Prinet, "Armorial de France," p. 22, No. 49, and Brault, *Eight Thirteenth Century Rolls of Arms*, p. 79, No. 49. For identification of the Grandpré blazon see Adam-Even and Jéquier, "Un Armorial français," p. 59, No. 853, and Brault, *Eight Thirteenth Century Rolls of Arms*, p. 47, No. 35.

7. Anselme de Saint-Marie, *Histoire généalogique et chronologique de la maison royale de France...*, 9 vols., 3rd ed. (Paris, 1726–1733; repr., Paris, 1967), 2:501, 6:716. William M. Newman, *Les Seigneurs de Nesle en Picardie, 12e siècle à 1286*, Memoirs of the American Philosophical Society 91, 2 pts. (Philadelphia, 1972), pt. 1:68, No. 31.

8. According to Anselme, *Histoire généalogique*, 2:317, 501, Yolande's paternal grandmother was Ade of Grandpré, dame de Hans, daughter of Henry IV, count of Grandpré, and the third wife of Raoul I, count of Soissons. Newman, *Les Seigneurs de Nesle*, pt. 1:66–68, Nos. 27–29, 31, believes that Ade was the widow, not the daughter of Henry IV of Grandpré and that her later marriage to Raoul I of Soissons produced no children that survived them. Newman also thinks that Yolande's father, Raoul, and his elder brother, Jean II, count of Soissons, were both sons of Raoul I and his second wife, a woman named Yolande whose family

A miniature in M729 helps to resolve the identity of one of the remaining coats of arms. The illustration before the beginning of Matins of the Virgin depicts a woman kneeling before an altar on which is placed a small statue of the Virgin and Child (fig. 19). The woman is formally dressed in a mantle that is decorated with the heraldic design, *or semy of lions passant and fretty gules.* This device matches one of the unidentified coats of arms from the border shields (Table 1b). Since the devices of lions and frets and the red and gold colors are probably adaptations from the Soissons arms, it is likely that this device was Yolande's personal coat of arms and that the miniature represents the prayer book's owner at her devotions.[9]

The importance of the heraldic evidence goes beyond the identification of M729's patron to place this manuscript in a geographical and historical context. All of Yolande's familial relations were established members of the northern French nobility. Yolande herself descended from

---

background is unknown. He bases this claim on two documents: an act of 21 March 1241, where Jean II describes his parents as "Le comte Raol mon père et la comtesse Yolant sa femme, ma mere," and another act of Jean II in May, 1233, where he speaks of his brother Raoul, Yolande's father, as "Radulphus, frater meus." Since the only evidence for determining the identity of Raoul's mother is the fact that he was Jean II's brother, either of Raoul I's wives, Yolande or Ade, remain possibilities. Because Raoul's daughter was named Yolande, it might indicate that Raoul's mother was also named Yolande, and thus Yolande's paternal grandmother would be Raoul I's second wife. The presence of the Grandpré coat of arms in M729 might indicate, on the other hand, that Yolande's paternal grandmother was Ade, Count Raoul I's third wife. With the available evidence, it is only possible to conclude that there was, in Yolande's genealogy, a relationship with the Grandpré family through her paternal grandfather's third wife, Ade.

9. This device does not correspond to the most common composition of women's coats of arms, in which the heraldic devices of a woman's husband and father were used. Rémi Mathieu, *Le Système héraldique français* (Paris, 1946), pp. 123–126. However, the composition of heraldic devices for women was flexible at this period, and there are many examples from the thirteenth century of various combinations of devices for women. Louis Bouly de Lesdain, "Les Armoiries des femmes d'après les sceaux," *Annuaire du Conseil héraldique de France* (1898), 176–196. The sixth coat of arms is *gules, a fess or.* The Bailleul and Saint-Omer families of Picardy as well as Gerars de Lauett, sire de Jauche in Brabant and sire de Baudour in Hainaut, bore this heraldic device. Prinet, "Armorial de France," p. 17, No. 46; Brault, *Eight Thirteenth Century Rolls of Arms,* p. 79, No. 46; Henri Jougla de Morenas, *Grand Armorial de France. Catalogue général des armoires des familles nobles de France* (Paris, 1934–53), p. 24; G. W. Watson, "Notes on the Foreign Coats of Arms in Planché's Roll of Arms," *The Genealogist,* n.s. 7 (1890), 38, No. 446. None of these families, however, has a demonstrable genealogical connection with Yolande of Soissons, so it is impossible to determine the exact identification of this blazon in M729.

the branch of the Nesle family of Picardy that became the counts of Soissons. Her grandfather was Raoul I, count of Soissons (1180–1235), and her uncle was Jean II, count of Soissons who died between 1270 and 1272.[10]

Yolande's father was Raoul of Soissons, the second son of Count Raoul I and brother of Count Jean II. He possibly held the title of vicomte of Coeuvres.[11] A knight who made at least two trips to the Holy Land, he was also a poet who composed several *chansons* in which he spoke of some of his adventures.[12] In 1239, he probably went to the Holy Land with Thibaut of Champagne, and at Acre he married Alix, queen of Cyprus and daughter of Henry II of Champagne, king of Jerusalem.[13] Alix was named regent of the kingdom of Jerusalem in 1242, but according to chroniclers, the weakness of her position caused her husband, Raoul of Soissons, to return to France "in disgust" because his power was "no more than that of a shadow."[14] Learning of Alix's death in 1246, Raoul married a lady from another Picard family, known only as Comtesse of Hangest who was the daughter of Jean I of Hangest.[15] He went back to the Holy Land on Louis IX's first crusade in 1248 and returned to France in 1253 or 1254.[16] In preparation for the second crusade with Louis IX, in 1270 he sold his right to the forest of Sec-Aunay, but whether he actually made this journey is uncertain.[17] He was still living in 1272, and the exact date of his death is unknown.[18]

There is little historical information about Yolande of Soissons. She

10. Newman, *Les Seigneurs de Nesle*, pt. 1:22–23 and the chart after p. 287.
11. Although Newman, *Les Seigneurs de Nesle*, pt. 1:68, No. 31, finds no evidence for connecting this title with Raoul of Soissons, the Morcuil heirs of Yolande of Soissons seem to have carried this title. Anselme, *Histoire généalogique*, 6:717.
12. Paulin Paris, "Chansonniers," *Histoire littéraire de la France*, 23 (Paris, 1856), pp. 700–705; E. Winkler, *Die Lieder Raouls von Soissons* (Halle, 1914).
13. Hans Eberhard Mayer, *The Crusades*, trans. John Gillingham (Oxford, 1972), pp. 234, 249; Jonathan Riley-Smith, *The Feudal Nobility and the Kingdom of Jerusalem, 1174–1277* (London, 1973), pp. 211–212.
14. *L'Estoire de Eracles empereur et la conqueste de la terre d'Outre Mer*, Recueil des historiens des Croisades, Historiens Occidentaux, 2 (Paris, 1859), p. 420; *Les Gestes des Chiprois*, Recueil des historiens des Croisades, Documents Arméniens, 2 (Paris, 1906), p. 735.
15. Anselme, *Histoire généalogique*, 6:738; Newman, *Les Seigneurs de Nesle*, pt. 1:68, No. 31.
16. L'abbé Pécheur, *Annales du diocèse de Soissons*, 3 (Soissons, 1875), p. 401; Joinville, *The Life of St. Louis*, trans. M. R. B. Shaw (Harmondsworth, 1963), p. 282.
17. Pécheur, *Annales du diocèse de Soissons*, 3:536.
18. Newman, *Les Seigneurs de Nesle*, pt. 1:68, Nos. 29, 31.

was the only known child of Raoul of Soissons and his wife, Comtesse of Hangest.[19] She was born either between this marriage in 1246 and 1248, when Raoul joined Louis IX on crusade, or after his return in 1253 or 1254. Yolande was married to Bernard V, seigneur of Moreuil by 1276 when both she and Bernard were mentioned as husband and wife in an act of Jean III, count of Soissons. In this act, Jean III called Yolande "nostre cousine."[20]

Yolande's marriage allied her with the Moreuil family of Picardy. The territory of Moreuil, located about twenty kilometers southeast of Amiens near the river Avre, originally developed around a town situated where a Roman road crossed the river.[21] This family was a vassal of the bishops of Amiens and was closely connected with the abbey of Corbie.[22] Originally the abbey owned this land, but in the early twelfth century, the abbey of Corbie established a seigneurie at Moreuil while retaining certain property and other rights there.[23] As evidence of their position, around 1127 Bernard, the first seigneur of Moreuil, built a château at Moreuil and was known as "dominus."[24] Through the twelfth and thirteenth centuries, the seigneurs of Moreuil extended their influence through their vassals in neighboring areas, and they maintained their feudal ties with the bishops of Amiens and the abbey of Corbie.[25]

Bernard V, Yolande's husband, was the seventh seigneur of Moreuil. His birth and death dates are unknown. He is first documented in 1259 when he settled certain agreements that his father had made with the abbey of Saint-Eloi. In 1289, he was one of the knights in the company of the count of Guelders. He was still living in 1302.[26]

Yolande of Soissons and Bernard of Moreuil had three sons and one daughter. Bernard VI, who inherited the seigneurie of Moreuil, played an active role in the affairs of France in the first half of the fourteenth century. In 1304, his earliest documented appearance, he confirmed an

19. Anselme, *Histoire généalogique*, 2:501; Newman, *Les Seigneurs de Nesle*, pt. 1:68, No. 31.
20. Newman, *Les Seigneurs de Nesle*, pt. 1:68, No. 31.
21. Robert Fossier, *La Terre et les hommes en Picardie jusqu'à la fin du 13e siècle* (Paris, 1968), pp. 118 n.21, 125, 704.
22. Ibid., p. 513.
23. Ibid., p. 704.
24. Ibid., p. 513.
25. Ibid., pp. 704–705, and the map between pp. 678–679; Anselme, *Histoire généalogique*, 6:716.
26. Anselme, *Histoire généalogique*, 6:716.

exemption that his uncle, Raoul of Soissons, had made. In 1314, he served Philip the Fair in conflicts with Flanders, and again, in 1337, Philip of Valois ordered him to assemble the Picard nobility at Amiens for war. After 1340, Bernard served as maréchal of France. He was still living in 1350.[27] Jean, known as seigneur of Plessis in 1286, appeared with Bernard VI in 1318 at Corbie to assist in the settlement of a dispute between the countess and the nobility of Artois. The date of his death is unknown.[28] The third son, Thibaut, seigneur of Coulombier and of Bretonniere, was first mentioned in 1325 when he acquired a rent on the land of Renicourt from the seigneur of Moy. He served the French king in wars in Flanders between 1337 and 1342 and was killed at the battle of Crecy in 1346.[29] Isabelle, their daughter, was married around 1300 to Ancel, seigneur of l'Isle-Adam.[30]

This evidence, although meager, presents a picture of Yolande as a lady of the northern French nobility. She grew up in the family of the counts of Soissons and maintained her connection with these relatives after her marriage.[31] As the wife of Bernard V, seigneur of Moreuil, she moved to another part of Picardy. She probably lived in the family residence built by Bernard I at Moreuil where her children likely were raised. Yolande's adult life undoubtedly was occupied with her duties as a mother and as the wife of a member of the Picard nobility whose feudal connections and sphere of influence were in Amiens and territories just south of this city.[32]

The historical situation of Yolande and her family sets a framework for dating M729. Because of the use of the Moreuil coat of arms, M729 was made at the time of or after Yolande's marriage. The only certain fact about Yolande's life is that by 1276 she was married to Bernard. Considering her possible birth dates, either between 1246 and 1248 or after 1253–1254, she could have been married before 1276. A date of around 1270 would mark a probable limit for the beginning of her married life.

27. Ibid., 6:714–717.
28. Ibid., 6:716.
29. Ibid., 6:716–717.
30. Ibid., 6:717.
31. Yolande and Bernard are mentioned in an act of Jean III, count of Soissons, in 1276. Newman, *Les Seigneurs de Nesle*, pt. 1:68, No. 31. Their son, Bernard VI, confirmed an agreement made by his uncle Raoul, son of Count Jean II of Soissons and Yolande's cousin. Anselme, *Histoire généalogique*, 6:714.
32. Fossier, *La Terre et les hommes*, p. 705. In the mid-thirteenth century, two seigneurs of Moreuil, Bernard III and IV, were known for making the Avre River navigable to Amiens. Anselme, *Histoire généalogique*, 6:716.

The lives of Yolande's children and husband provide the only other guideposts for determining anything about her activities or the length of her life. Her son Jean, probably the second child, was living in 1286 when he was known as seigneur of Plessis.[33] Isabelle, her daughter and possibly the youngest child, was married around 1300, establishing a likely date for her birth around 1280 or slightly later.[34] Two of her sons, Bernard VI and Thibaut, were active into the mid-fourteenth century; Bernard, probably the eldest, was still living in 1350. Considering a possible life span for Bernard, the title of Jean in 1286, and the marriage of Isabelle around 1300, it is likely that the four children were born in the years between around 1270 and 1285. Yolande's husband was still living in 1302, but he may have died by 1304.[35] This chronology indicates that Yolande's most active mature years can be placed between 1270 and 1300, and the acquisition of her sumptuous prayer book probably falls within this same thirty-year time span.

Two miniatures in the Psalter and Hours of Yolande of Soissons must also be considered for their possible contribution to a more specific dating of M729. One of these illuminations is the full-page miniature that faces the beginning of Matins in the Hours of the Virgin (fig. 19). The woman kneeling at a prie-dieu placed in front of an altar has already been identi-

33. In Anselme's genealogy in the *Histoire généalogique*, 6:716, Jean is listed as the first son and Bernard VI as the second son. The description of M729 in William D. Wixom, *Treasures from Medieval France* (Cleveland, 1967), p. 168, follows this order. A later genealogy by de la Chesnaye-DeBois, *Dictionnaire de la noblesse*, 14 (Paris, 1867), p. 557, lists Bernard as the eldest and Jean as the second son. This order is probably correct because if Jean, who was living in 1318, had been the eldest son, he would have inherited the seigneurie of Moreuil. The fact that he was named seigneur of Plessis also probably indicates that he was being provided with other titles and territory as a younger son. The age at which Jean became seigneur of Plessis would help to establish his birth date and thus provide some information for dating M729. It is difficult to arrive at a satisfactory solution to this problem, however. Although there seems to have been no established age at which a boy could receive a title, fifteen or sixteen was considered a marriageable age. In the thirteenth century, twenty may have been considered a more usual transition point into manhood. For some of these problems concerning age and generations in the Middle Ages see David Herlihy, "The Generation in Medieval History," *Viator. Medieval and Renaissance Studies* 5 (1974), 352–355.

34. A date of around 1280 assumes that she was between the ages of fifteen and twenty when she married. Anselme, *Histoire généalogique*, 6:717, lists Isabelle fourth in the genealogy.

35. In 1304, his son, Bernard VI, confirmed an agreement made by his uncle, Raoul of Soissons. See n. 31, above. It is possible that, since his father did not participate in this act, he had died and Bernard VI had inherited the seigneurie.

fied as the manuscript's owner, the lady Yolande, but the artist uses outward symbols such as the heraldic device on her fur-lined mantle rather than a physical likeness to identify the person portrayed.[36] This conventional representation therefore adds no evidence for dating M729.

The second picture is the first miniature in the prefatory cycle (fig. 1a). It depicts a man standing on the left in front of a gate. He holds a pair of gloves in one hand and places his other hand on a woman's shoulder. This woman stands to the right. She looks back at the man while placing her hands on the shoulders of two boys in front of her. The miniature appears to depict a family group clothed in typical late-thirteenth-century dress.[37] This illumination has been identified as a portrait of Yolande of Soissons with her husband, Bernard, and two of their sons.[38] The only evidence for this identification comes from the heraldic devices placed around the border of this illustration, combined with the figures' contemporary attire. When the miniature is placed within the context of the manuscript's complete iconographic program, however, the probability of the identification is increased. In M729, every miniature and historiated initial has a clear function in illustrating its accompanying text, and the prefatory cycle, though lacking a specific textual base, conforms to a pattern of prefatory Psalter illustration with its depiction of two saints and a short Christological cycle.[39] The family portrait fits into this scheme by expressing their particular veneration of the saints who are illustrated in the following two miniatures, and the placement of this group at the beginning of the manuscript may have served as a visual identification for the original owner that enhanced the devotional purpose of the prayer book.[40]

36. For the identity of the coat of arms on her mantle see p. 4.
37. All four people wear tunics with sleeves fitting tightly at the wrist under a surcoat with fuller sleeves that fit in between the elbow and wrist. The man's surcoat is slit up the front, and the woman wears a wimple and veil on her head. The men wear shaped shoes with pointed toes. For comparisons see Joan Evans, *Dress in Medieval France* (Oxford, 1952), pp. 14–24; Cecil Willett and Phillis Cunnington, *Handbook of English Medieval Costume* (London, 1960), pp. 42–53.
38. Wixom, *Treasures from Medieval France*, p. 168.
39. See Chapter III, p. 68.
40. For a possible rearrangement of the two saints' miniatures and its relationship to the family miniature see Chapter III, pp. 111–114. I have pursued the possibility that this miniature represents a biblical subject. One incident that corresponds in the number of people and the action of leaving a walled gate is the account in Ruth 1.1–2 where Elimelech, his wife Naomi, and their two sons leave Bethlehem to go to the country of Moab. The identification of the M729 miniature as this subject is unlikely for two reasons. First, while the coincidence of the number of

As in the portrait of Yolande alone, the figure style and facial definition in the family miniature follow conventional types found throughout the manuscript's illustrations. The artist does not attempt a physical likeness of the persons portrayed, so it is impossible to judge the ages of these people from this illustration.[41] However, only two boys are depicted, and since Yolande and Bernard had four children, this detail might suggest that the miniature was painted before the birth of the third son and the daughter, providing a date of around 1275 to 1280 for this illumination.[42] Two other interpretations qualify the accuracy of this date. First, it is possible that the other children had been born but were too young to be included in this family scene. In this case, the possible date could be expanded into

figures and the presence of a city or gate provides a similarity between the M729 miniature and representations of Elimelech's departure, significant details differ. For example, as in a portion of a Bible in the library at Troyes, MS 106, the family is usually wearing traveling garments such as a hat and staff with knapsack for Elimelech, mantles for the children, and a shawl covering Naomi's head and shoulders. See Lucien Morel-Payen, *Les Plus Beaux Manuscrits et les plus belles reliures de la Bibliothèque de Troyes* (Troyes, 1935), p. 101, fig. 59. Second, unless other miniatures are missing from the prefatory cycle, this Old Testament subject does not fit into the iconographic program of the prefatory cycle or the remainder of the manuscript. However, it is possible that the artist of the M729 miniature could have turned to a biblical scene such as the Elimelech episode for compositional inspiration since the M729 family miniature presented the problem of illustrating a relatively unprecedented secular scene. For the frequent compositional interchange between secular and religious subjects see M. Alison Stones, "Secular Manuscript Illumination in France," *Medieval Manuscripts and Textual Criticism* (Chapel Hill, 1976), pp. 95–96.

41. Wixom, *Treasures from Medieval France,* p. 168, states that "Judging by the combined evidence of the relative ages of Yolande and her family . . . together with the style of the miniatures, the greater part of the manuscript may be tentatively dated circa 1290." D. H. Turner, "The Development of Maître Honoré," *The Eric George Millar Bequest of Manuscripts and Drawings, 1967* (London, 1968), p. 57, says that "A recent proposal that evidence for a date can be drawn from the ages of Yolande and her family as they appear in a miniature on fol. 1b may be dismissed as entirely gratuitous. The 'portraits' are simply conventional, or, at the most, idealized representations, as they might be expected to be at the period." The existence of this family "portrait," however, demands that it not be dismissed entirely from considerations concerning the date of M729 on other grounds.

42. A date between 1275 and 1280 is based on two assumptions. First, the date of Isabelle's marriage about 1300 and the possibility that she was the youngest child could place her birth and perhaps Thibaut's (the third son) in the years around 1280. Second, if Jean was a child (approximately between ages five and ten) when this miniature was painted, these dates would make it possible for him to be in his teens by the time he was known as seigneur of Plessis in 1286.

the decade of the 1280s. In another view, the miniature might commemorate an event prior to the time when it was painted, and then its precise date could not be determined. Even accepting a date between around 1275 and the early 1280s for this particular miniature, the illumination of the remainder of the manuscript could have been in progress both before and after this illustration was painted. The balance of the historical documentation and portrait evidence in M729, however, suggests a date between 1275 and 1285 as a likely time for the production of this manuscript.

Although the origins of this Psalter and Hours in late-thirteenth-century Picardy can be established, only a partial record of the subsequent history of M729 can be reconstructed. By the late fourteenth century the manuscript was in the hands of Charles of Poitiers, who was elected to the bishopric of Poitiers on January 30, 1390, as the verse on folio 434v indicates.[43] It is probable that the office dedicated to St. Michael (fols. 404–433) was added while Charles owned the manuscript. The script and illumination of this section is characteristic of the late fourteenth or early fifteenth century. The script of the verse is also consistent with this date.[44]

There is no other trace of the manuscript's provenance until it appeared in the collection of William Young Ottley (1771–1836), a collector and historian of art as well as an amateur artist. In the sale of the Ottley collection at Sotheby's in 1838, the Psalter and Hours appeared in two lots, one consisting of twenty miniatures and the other containing the rest of the manuscript. Sir Frederic Madden, then the head of the Department of Manuscripts at the British Museum, recognized that the twenty miniatures had been removed from the Psalter and recommended that they be sold together. The book firm of Payne and Foss bought the manu-

---

43. The verse is:

> L'an mil ccc. deus fois quarante
> Et x. in Ianvier des iours trente
> Fust promoncies ie vous raconte
> K. di Poitiers evesque et comte.

The script of the verse is in the same hand as some of the marginal corrections for the *Dame resplendisans* on fols. 220r and v, 221v. Charles of Poitiers died in 1433. Anselme, *Histoire généalogique*, 2:199, 218. The illuminations in the Office of St. Michael are: Michael casting Lucifer from heaven, a miniature on fol. 404v; two historiated initials, the Coronation of the Virgin (fol. 405r) and Christ in Majesty (fol. 427r). There are six large decorated initials and ornamented borders.

44. Wixom, *Treasures from Medieval France*, p. 168.

script after the Sotheby sale and subsequently sold it to Robert Stayner Holford.[45]

Holford, whose collections at Westonbirt in Gloucestershire and Dorchester House in London included fine printed books, paintings, and prints, was among the British collectors who recognized the importance of including manuscript illumination among other types of art in their collections.[46] When Gustav Waagen was preparing his book, *Treasures of Art in Great Britain,* he examined Holford's holdings and included a description of the Psalter and Hours of Yolande of Soissons among his record of the works of art from this collection.[47] After Robert Holford's death in 1892, his collection remained in the possession of his son, Sir George Holford. The Psalter and Hours was exhibited at the Burlington Fine Arts Club in 1908 and was included in a description of the Holford collection.[48] After George Holford's death in 1926, the Pierpont Morgan Library acquired some of the Holford manuscripts including the Psalter and Hours of Yolande of Soissons, now M729.[49]

Since twenty miniatures were separated from the Psalter and Hours of Yolande of Soissons while part of the Ottley collection, the original arrangement of the manuscript has been disrupted, and when the manuscript was in the Holford collection, the order of the folios differed from the present one. In addition, two miniatures and part of the text are missing.[50] Before the manuscript was rebound in 1927, E. G. Millar carefully studied the sequence of the text and miniatures, and its present arrangement is the result of these efforts. The reconstruction reflects, on the whole, the original order of the Psalter and Hours, although examina-

45. Alan Noel Latimer Munby, *Connoisseurs and Medieval Miniatures, 1750–1850* (Oxford, 1972), pp. 62–68.
46. Munby, *Connoisseurs,* pp. 147–150.
47. Gustav F. Waagen, *Treasures of Art in Great Britain,* 2 (London, 1854), pp. 206–208.
48. Burlington Fine Arts Club, *Exhibition of Illuminated Manuscripts* (London, 1908), pp. 65–66, pl. 94; Sir George Holford, *The Holford Collection* (London, 1924), p. 37, pls. 8, 9.
49. Munby, *Connoisseurs,* pp. 148–149.
50. Munby, *Connoisseurs,* p. 68. The description in Waagen, *Treasures of Art,* reflects some of these differences. The miniatures before Psalm 1 and Matins of the Holy Spirit are missing. The first part of the text at Matins of the Holy Spirit is also gone. The Pierpont Morgan Library kindly allowed me to see the notes made before the rebinding, which include a description of the former arrangement of the manuscript.

tion of the iconographical cycles suggests that alternate arrangements may, in a few cases, be possible.[51]

THE TEXT

The Psalter and Hours of Yolande of Soissons is a prayer book that combines two types of texts used for private devotions by the laity, the Psalter and the Book of Hours. In M729, a calendar that precedes the Psalter begins the text, while canticles with a litany follow (see Appendix A). In the Book of Hours portion, the Hours of the Virgin and the Hours of the Holy Spirit combine in alternating sections, and the Hours of the Cross come after these offices. The Seven Penitential Psalms, the Office of the Dead, and the Psalter of St. Jerome complete the Book of Hours. Throughout the manuscript, numerous prayers and verses are interspersed.

Although the contents of M729 are typical of these devotional books, several aspects of this text deserve special notice. First, the combination of the Psalter and the Book of Hours represents a transition in the text of extra-liturgical books of the Middle Ages. From the early medieval period through the thirteenth century, the Psalter, often with calendar, litany, and various prayers, was the standard private devotional book.[52] During this time, however, the religious orders were developing additions to the Divine Office that would become the basic components of the Book of Hours. These new elements included groups of Psalms, such as the Seven Penitential Psalms, and offices that expressed special devotion, for example to the Virgin, the Cross, or the Holy Spirit.[53] The recitation of these extra elements spread to the secular clergy and the laity, for whom the invariable daily repetition and the humanizing expression of religious senti-

---

51. See Chapter III, pp. 69, 111–112.
52. Edgar Hoskins, *Horae beatae Mariae virginis or Sarum and York Primers* (London, 1901), pp. vi–xi. For examples of Psalters as devotional books see Victor Leroquais, *Les Psautiers manuscrits latins des bibliothèques publiques de France*, 3 vols. (Macon, 1940–41), and Günther Haseloff, *Die Psalterillustration im 13. Jahrhundert: Studien zur Geschichte der Buchmalerei in England, Frankreich und den Niederlanden* (Kiel, 1938).
53. Edmund Bishop, "On the Origin of the Prymer," *Liturgica Historica* (Oxford, 1918), pp. 214–228; *Horae Eboracenses*, Publication of the Surtees Society for 1919 (Durham, 1920), pp. xv–xxvi; Victor Leroquais, *Les Livres d'heures manuscrits de la Bibliothèque Nationale*, 1 (Paris, 1927), p. ix; E. S. Dewick, *Facsimiles of Horae de Beata Maria Virgine from English MSS. of the Eleventh Century*, Henry Bradshaw Society Publications 21 (London, 1902).

ment in the special devotional offices had wide appeal. From the middle of the thirteenth century, this new type of devotional book with the office or Hours of the Virgin as its core had become established and began to supplant the Psalter as the prayer book for the laity. The small number of extant Psalter-Hours texts of which M729 is an example demonstrate the transitional stage of this important change.[54]

The text itself provides information about localization of the manuscript. Liturgical variations may indicate that a Book of Hours was designed for the use of a particular diocese or city. Examination of the Hours of the Virgin in M729 for localization on the basis of usage, however, yields inconclusive results (see Table 2). While most of the sections follow Sarum usage, there are mixtures of texts characteristic of Paris, Reims, Châlons-sur-Marne, Amiens, Chartres, Orleans, and Lyons. While the relatively early position of M729 in the development of Books of Hours texts may explain some of these inconsistencies, it is only possible to conclude that the Hours of the Virgin in the Psalter and Hours of Yolande of Soissons were composed for a usage different from Paris, Rome, or Sarum.[55]

A study of the saints in the calendar provides the clearest localization of M729 (see Appendix B). A script of either red or blue designates major feasts of the church, the apostles, and other saints of special veneration.[56] Several saints in this third category demonstrate that this calendar is based on Amiens usage. A number of these saints are of Amiens origin. On September 25, the calendar records in blue the feast of Firmin I, the first bishop of Amiens, with an octave on 2 October. Firminus II, the third bishop of Amiens, who built a church on the site of St. Firmin I's grave, appears in blue on 1 September. Victoricus, Fuscianus, and Gentianus, who were martyred near Amiens, are inscribed in red on December 11, and Honoratus (Honoré), the bishop of Amiens who discovered their bodies and to whom the south portal of Amiens Cathedral is dedicated, is recorded

---

54. Bishop, "On the Origin of the Prymer," pp. 231–247; Leroquais, *Les Livres d'heures,* 1:x; L. M. J. Delaissé, "The Importance of Books of Hours for the History of the Medieval Book," *Gatherings in Honor of Dorothy E. Miner* (Baltimore, 1974), pp. 203–204.

55. Leroquais, *Les Livres d'heures,* 1:xxviii–xxxix; Montague Rhodes James, *A Descriptive Catalogue of Manuscripts in the Fitzwilliam Museum* (Cambridge, 1895), pp. xxvii–xxix, xxxv–xxxvi.

56. Although this principle is not applied with complete consistency, each color seems to indicate a different degree of solemnity, with blue marking the most important feasts.

Table 2: USAGE OF THE HOURS OF THE VIRGIN, M729

Matins	Hymn: Quem terra, fol. 233r	Rome or Sarum
	Antiphon: Benedicta tu, fol. 234v	Rome or Sarum
	Lesson I: Sancta Maria virgo virginum, fol. 236v	Sarum
	Lesson II: Sancta Maria piarum piissima, fol. 237r	Sarum
	Lesson III: Sancta Maria Dei genitrix, fol. 237v	Sarum
	Lesson IV: O regina scala celi thronus, fol. 240v	—
	Lesson V: Dele virgo beatissima nostra, fol. 241r	
	Lesson VI: Placatus precibus virgo, fol. 241r	—
	Lesson VII: O beata Maria, fol. 244v	Chartres, Lyons, Orleans
	Lesson VIII: Admitte piissima virgo, fol. 244v	Chartres, Lyons, Orleans
	Lesson IX: Sancta Maria succurre miseris, fol. 245r	Chartres, Lyons, Orleans
Lauds	Antiphon: O admirabile, fol. 247r	Sarum
	Capitulum: Virgo verbo concepit, fol. 252v	Reims, Châlons - sur-Marne
	Hymn: O gloriosa domina, fol. 252v	Rome or Sarum
	Antiphon: O gloriosa Dei genitrix, fol. 253r	Sarum
Prime	Hymn: Veni creator, fol. 268r	Paris or Sarum
	Antiphon: O admirabile, fol. 268v	Sarum
	Capitulum: Hec est virgo, fol. 270v	Amiens
Tierce	Hymn: Veni sancte Spiritus, fol. 276r	—
	Antiphon: Quando natus, fol. 276r	Sarum
	Capitulum: Paradisi porta, fol. 277v	Paris
Sext	Hymn: Veni creator, fol. 283r	Paris or Sarum
	Antiphon: Rubum quem, fol. 283v	Sarum
	Capitulum: Gaude Maria virgo, fol. 284r	Paris
Nones	Hymn: Veni creator, fol. 290r	Paris or Sarum
	Antiphon: Germinavit, fol. 290v	Sarum
	Capitulum: Per te Dei genitrix, fol. 291r	Paris
Vespers	Antiphon: Beata mater, fol. 299v	—
	Capitulum: Beata es, fol. 299v	Paris or Sarum
	Hymn: Ave maris stella, fol. 300r	Rome
	Antiphon: Sancta Maria, fol. 301r	Paris or Sarum
Compline	Antiphon: Cum iocunditate, fol. 306r	Sarum
	Hymn: Virgo Dei genitrix	Paris
	Capitulum: Sicut cynamomum, fol. 308r	Paris or Sarum
	Antiphon: Ecce completa sunt, fol. 308v	—

on 16 May in blue. The bodies of the two Saint Firmins, Honoré, and Fuscien were the major relics in Amiens Cathedral.[57]

Other saints whose names are highlighted in red or blue in the calendar were important in the Amiens liturgy. In M729, St. Martin of Tours appears twice; his feast day on November 11 and the translation of his relics on 4 July are both inscribed in red. St. Martin was especially venerated in Amiens because the famous incident of Martin dividing his cloak took place there. An oratory was built in Amiens to mark the place where this event occurred. By the thirteenth century, this oratory had become the abbey of Saint-Martin-aux-Jumeaux and was located inside the cloister to the south of Amiens Cathedral.[58] A church just beside this abbey, also inside the cloister area, was dedicated to St. Nicholas, a popular saint throughout Picardy.[59] The calendar of M729 records St. Nicholas on December 6 in red. The titular saint of an Amiens church founded by the cathedral chapter was St. Laurence, and this saint also is designated in red in the M729 calendar, on August 10 with an octave on 17 August.[60]

Two important saints from Reims, Remigius (Remi), the bishop of Reims who baptized Clovis I (October 1, in red), and Nichasius (Nicaise), the first archbishop of Reims (December 14, in red), receive a special place in the calendar of M729. Since the diocese of Amiens was part of the archbishopric of Reims, the appearance of these two saints would not be unusual in an Amiens calendar, but there is additional evidence for their veneration in this city. One of the chapels in the choir of Amiens Cathedral was dedicated to St. Nicaise, and St. Remi was the titular saint of a parish church in Amiens that was under the jurisdiction of the cathedral chapter.[61]

Special circumstances enhanced the position at Amiens of two of the four remaining saints in this category. The beheading of John the Baptist (August 29, in blue) gained particular meaning at Amiens since the cathe-

---

57. See the calendar in Georges Durand, *Ordinaire de l'eglise Notre-Dame cathedrale d'Amiens par Raoul de Rouvroy (1291),* Mémoires de la Société des Antiquaires de Picardie, Documents inédits concernant la province, 22 (Amiens, 1934), pp. 1–20. The relics of these saints were placed behind and beneath the main altar. See Durand, *Ordinaire,* pp. xxx–xxxi.

58. The abbey was under the jurisdiction of the cathedral chapter. Durand, *Ordinaire,* pp. xlii–xliii.

59. Durand, *Ordinaire,* p. xliii.

60. Durand, *Ordinaire,* p. xlv.

61. Durand, *Ordinaire,* pp. xxxviii–xxxix, xlv–xlvi, pl. 1. The chapel was on the south side of the chevet, designated as number XXIV on the plan (pl. 1).

dral at Amiens acquired a relic of John the Baptist's head in 1206. One of the choir chapels was dedicated to this saint.[62] Although Thomas, archbishop of Canterbury (December 29, in blue), was often designated for special veneration in medieval calendars, from the end of the twelfth century close connections were established between the monks at Canterbury and the canons of Amiens Cathedral—the monks instituted an anniversary in their church for the Amiens canons, who reciprocated the gesture.[63] Only Saints Gervasius and Prothasius (June 19, in red), patrons of Soissons, and St. Sylvester (December 31, in red) lack discernible ties with Amiens.

Other saints recorded in the regular brown ink add to the evidence for an Amiens localization. Two additional feasts for the saints of special veneration are mentioned: on January 14, where the inscription of the name Firminus refers to the feast of St. Firmin I's invention, and on May 9, the translation of the relics of St. Nicholas.[64] Walaricus (Valeric), founder of the monastery of Leuconay in the diocese of Amiens, appears twice, with his feast day on 1 April and the translation of his relics on 12 December. Other saints associated with Amiens include Richarius (Riquier), whose relics were brought to the abbey of Saint-Riquier at Centula, near Amiens (April 26), and Quintinus (Quentin), who was martyred near Amiens (October 3). A choir chapel in the cathedral at Amiens was dedicated to St. Quentin.[65] On June 25, the calendar records the translation of relics of St. Eligius (Eloi). As bishop of Noyon and Tournai, he was associated most closely with these areas in northern France. However, he was

---

62. For the acquisition of this relic see Jules Corblet, *Hagiographie du diocèse d'Amiens*, 5 (Paris, 1869–75), p. 65; Durand, *Ordinaire*, pp. xxxv–xxxvi. The reception of this relic, celebrated on 17 December, is not recorded in the M729 calendar. The chapel is on the north side of the chevet, number XXIII.

63. Durand, *Ordinaire*, pp. xxxvi–xxxvii.

64. The discovery of St. Firmin's body actually was celebrated on 13 January. The reason for the change of date in M729 is unclear. On January 13, the M729 calendar records saints Hilary and Remi, whose feasts on this date were not mentioned in the Amiens Cathedral ordinal of 1291. Durand, *Ordinaire*, p. 1. The inclusion of Hilary and Remi, regardless of the reason, does not explain the inscription of St. Firmin on the following day since the M729 calendar records separate feasts on the same date in other places (January 25, May 3, July 21, August 9, October 1, October 31, November 29, December 13). This alteration of the date may reflect a desire to separate St. Firmin's invention from the octave of the Epiphany, also on 13 January. Between 1304 and 1306, a new office was instituted in Amiens for the feast of St. Firmin's invention in order to emphasize its importance apart from the octave. The date, however, was not changed. Durand, *Ordinaire*, pp. xiv, xvii.

65. Chapel XXI on the north side of the chevet. Durand, *Ordinaire*, p. xxxv, pl. 1.

also an important saint at Amiens because he discovered the relics of St. Quentin. One of the choir chapels of Amiens Cathedral was dedicated to St. Eloi.[66]

Although the M729 calendar places an emphasis on saints venerated at Amiens, the interests of the patrons of this manuscript explain the presence of some of the other saints. The calendar includes, for example, a number of Soissons saints. Gervasius and Prothasius, the patrons of Soissons, are highlighted in red on 19 June. Crispinus and Crispianus, also patrons of Soissons, are commemorated on 25 October. Medard and Gildard, whose relics were in the abbey of Saint-Médard-de-Soissons appear in the calendar on June 8. Valerius and Rufinus (June 14) and Benedicta (October 8), all martyred near Soissons, are other saints from this area. These saints from Soissons were probably included for the original owner, Yolande, a descendant of the counts of Soissons.

Another saint, Vedast (Vaast), bishop of Arras and Cambrai, has three different celebrations recorded in this calendar: his feast day on February 6, the *relatio* on July 15, and on October 1, the translation of his relics. The appearance of all three of these feasts is unusual except in manuscripts made for the abbey of Saint-Vaast at Arras.[67] There was, however, an abbey dedicated to St. Vedast at Moreuil that Bernard I, seigneur of Moreuil, founded in the early twelfth century.[68] The presence of three feasts honoring St. Vedast in M729's calendar probably reflects the continued patronage that the seigneurs of Moreuil gave to this abbey.

The saints in the litany and the suffrages add little to the evidence for localization. The saints invoked in the litany follow, in general, a pattern of saints often appearing in this section (Appendix C). Of special interest are two German saints: Cunibert, a seventh-century bishop of Cologne,

---

66. Chapel XXII on the south side of the chevet. Durand, *Ordinaire*, p. xxxix, pl. 1. The M729 calendar records only St. Eloi's translation. On his feast day, December 1, Constantianus, abbot of Javron in the diocese of Mans whose relics were transferred from Le Mans to Breteuil, diocese of Beauvais, is commemorated. The calendar of the 1291 ordinal records only St. Eloi on 1 December. Durand, *Ordinaire*, p. 19.

67. See a Psalter from Saint-Vaast d'Arras of the early fourteenth century (Arras, Bibliothèque Municipale, MS 88) in Leroquais, *Les Psautiers*, 1:37, and an ordinal of Saint-Vaast of the early fourteenth century (Arras, Bibliothèque Municipale, MS 230[907]) in Louis Brou, *The Monastic Ordinale of St. Vedast's Abbey, Arras*, Henry Bradshaw Society Publications, 86 and 87 (London, 1957), 86:114.

68. Paul André Roger, *Archives historiques et ecclésiastiques de la Picardie et de l'Artois* (Amiens, 1842), p. 163 n.2, records the date of 1109 for the founding of this abbey. Anselme, *Histoire généalogique*, 6:715, gives the date as 1119.

and Afra, who was martyred at Augsburg. Other unusual saints in the litany are Gertrude, abbess of the monastery of Nivelles in Belgium; Orotildis, probably Rotrude, an alleged sister of Charlemagne whose relics were in Flanders; and Columba, possibly to be identified with the patroness of Sainte-Colombe at Sens.[69]

The suffrages repeat many of the saints that the calendar emphasized (Appendix D). Two of the three martyrs are Laurence and Nicaise, and Martin, Nicholas, and Eligius (Eloi) are the three confessors. St. James the Greater, to whom one of the chapels in Amiens Cathedral probably was dedicated, is also invoked.[70] St. Elizabeth, who is not recorded in either the calendar or litany, deserves special mention. A member of the Third Order of St. Francis, she was canonized in 1231. Her invocation in the suffrages provides a *terminus post quem* for the manuscript and underscores an interest in Franciscan themes that recurs in the iconography of the illustrations.

The inclusion of the legendary prayer with which St. Gilles (Aegidus) interceded for the forgiveness of an unconfessed sin of Charlemagne (Appendix A, fol. 208v) may bear some relationship to the northern French origins of M729. Although prayers to St. Gilles and pilgrimages to his shrine near Arles became popular from at least the tenth century, this saint was especially favored in the Picard region, where many churches were dedicated to him in the twelfth and thirteenth centuries.[71] Several French romances, probably of Picard authorship, also tell of pilgrimages that people from this region made to St. Gilles's shrine.[72] The popularity of this saint in Picardy may explain the presence of this prayer in M729.

69. Since the litany records only the saint's name and not the feast, it is not always possible to determine which saint was intended if there is more than one saint with a particular name. Gertrude could also be identified with a woman of this name who was martyred at Vaux-en-Dieulet in the diocese of Reims or an alleged sister of Charlemagne who retired to the cloister of Karlsberg on the Main. Frederick George Holweck, *A Biographical Dictionary of the Saints* (St. Louis, 1924), p. 432. Holweck, p. 226, lists twelve other saints named Columba most of whom were early Christian martyrs. Orotildis possibly could be identified with Rictrude who, with the help of St. Amand, founded and was abbess of the monastery of Marchiennes in Flanders. Holweck, *A Biographical Dictionary*, p. 858.

70. Chapel XXVI on the south side of the chevet. Durand, *Ordinaire*, p. xxxviii, pl. 1.

71. Frederick Brittain, *Saint Giles* (Cambridge, 1928), pp. 27–32; E. C. Jones, *Saint Gilles: Essai d'histoire littéraire* (Paris, 1914), p. 74. For a discussion of the cult of Saint Gilles see Ernest Rembry, *Saint Gilles: Sa Vie, ses reliques, son culte en Belgique et dans le nord de la France* (Bruges, 1881).

72. Jones, *Saint Gilles*, pp. 73–74.

Another significant textual aspect is the use of Old French in several prayers and verses. Because the prayers and poetry found in Books of Hours vary widely, they reflect not only the use of these manuscripts for personal devotion but also, on occasion, the taste and selection of a patron. The use of the vernacular brings an immediacy to these selections not found in the traditional Latin passages.[73] In addition, analysis of the dialect provides other information for localizing M729.

In the Psalter and Hours of Yolande of Soissons, there are several different types of texts in Old French. The rubrics that precede four prayers in both Latin and French offer brief instructions and explanations concerning these devotions (see Appendix A). Two longer prayers in prose entreat for help and defense from the temptations of daily life and request blessing and benediction (fols. 207r–208v). Two poems, the Fifteen Joys of the Virgin (fols. 217r–220r) and the *Dame resplendisans* (fols. 220r–222r), complete the Old French texts in M729. Both of these verses demonstrate the devotion to the Virgin that was ardent and widespread in the later Middle Ages.[74]

The Joys of the Virgin was a popular devotional text from at least the thirteenth century, as its many versions in verse and prose attest, but the *Dame resplendisans* may have been included in the Psalter and Hours of Yolande of Soissons for a special reason. Gautier de Coinci is the accepted author for this prayer to the Virgin in verse form. Born in the late twelfth century, Gautier entered the abbey of Saint-Médard-de-Soissons in 1193. He spent most of his life as prior of Vic-sur-Aisne, near Soissons, and for three years before his death in 1236 he was grand prior of Saint-Médard. His main literary contribution was a collection of miracles of the Virgin Mary, but Gautier also wrote a number of pious *chansons* and prayers, of which the *Dame resplendisans* is an example.[75] This poem, written in

73. Leroquais, *Les Livres d'heures*, 1:xxix. Edith Brayer, "Livres d'heures contenant des textes en français," *Bulletin d'Information de l'Institut de Recherche et d'Histoire des Textes* 12 (1963), 31.
74. For a transcription of the Old French texts in M729 see Gould, "The Psalter and Hours of Yolande of Soissons," pp. 284–296.
75. Arlette P. Ducrot-Granderye, *Etudes sur "Les Miracles de Nostre Dame" de Gautier de Coinci*, Annales Academiae Scientiarum Fennicae, B-25 (Helsinki, 1932), pp. 140–154; V. Frederic Koenig, *"Les Miracles de Nostre Dame" par Gautier de Coinci*, 4 vols. (Geneva, 1955–70). Koenig numbers the poems according to book number (Roman numeral), type of work (Mir for Miracle, ch for *chanson*, etc.), and relative position in that book (Arabic numeral). Ducrot-Granderye numbers the works consecutively. Koenig gives these numbers in parentheses as D.1, D.2, etc.

rhymed quatrains, speaks of the Virgin in terms such as "roïne glorieuse," "douce dame," and "fluns de misericorde" that illustrate a variety of conceptions about Notre Dame, from the Queen of Heaven to the compassionate mediatrix. The prayer is filled with images of the author as a sinner, "cest dolante pecheour," of his horror of the devil, "en infer sera m'ame du dragon devouree," and of his supplication to the Virgin for protection and intercession, "desfendés moi du diable." All these ideas relate to the themes of the longer miracles recorded in Gautier's collection.

Because Gautier was from the area of Soissons and was a monk at Saint-Médard, a lady from Soissons might select one of his prayers for her Psalter and Book of Hours. There is, however, an even closer connection between Gautier de Coinci and the family of Yolande of Soissons. Raoul I, count of Soissons and Yolande's paternal grandfather, was one of Gautier's associates among the laity. Gautier relates in one of his miracles how Raoul I informed him about the occasion when Raoul's father, Ives de Nesle, had witnessed Notre Dame of Soissons's miraculous healing of the face of the lady Gondree.[76] Gautier was also a friend of Ade, Raoul I's third wife and possibly Yolande's grandmother. He names her in the miracles of Notre Dame of Soissons, a work that Ade requested Gautier to write, and he also mentions her in his epilogue of Book II of the Mircles.[77] These connections between Gautier de Coinci and Yolande's paternal

---

76. Gautier de Coinci, *Les Miracles de Nostre Dame,* II. Mir 24 (D. 73), lines 662–665, ed. V. Frederic Koenig (Geneva, 1970), 4:242.

> Et li bons cuens, Raous m'a dit
> De Soissons qu'assez li conta
> Li cuens Yves qu'il li baisa
> Le nes plus de cinquante fois.

77. Gautier de Coinci, *Les Miracles de Nostre Dame,* II Mir 22 (D. 70–71), lines 14–19 and II Epi 33 (D. 81), lines 126–133, ed. Koenig, 4:190, 436.

> Mais pour ce un peu en sui engrans
> Que la contesse Ade m'en prie
> De Soissonz, qui mout est m'amie
> Et qui mout aimme de cuer fin
> La mere Dieu, qui bonne fin
> Li daint donner et bone vie . . .
>
> A röynes ou a duchoises,
> Qu'a a salüer pas ne m'oublies
> Mes deus especïaus amies,
> Mes deus contesses, mes deus dames,
> Des queles daint metre les ames
> En paradys li roys des roys.
> L'une est la contesse de Blois,
> Et l'autre est cele de Soissons.

grandparents make it very probable that the prayer, *Dame resplendisans,* was included in the Psalter and Hours of Yolande of Soissons especially for the owner of the manuscript, Yolande.

While the inclusion of the poem, *Dame resplendisans,* reflects a close association with Yolande of Soissons, the particular dialect of this prayer and the other Old French texts in M729 helps to localize this manuscript. Phonetical and morphological analysis demonstrates that the Old French portions of M729 were transcribed in Picard. Some of the Picard phonetical characteristics include the absence of the consonants *d* or *b* in the secondary groups, *n'r, m'l, l'r* as in *vinrent, sanle, humle;* the use of the verb form *caïr, kaïr,* for example in *meskiece;* and the use of *orison* and *pisson* for *oreison* and *peisson.* Among the morphological characteristics are the use of *le* for the feminine singular definite article, subject and *régime* cases; the appearance of *men, ten, sen* for the masculine singular possessive adjective; and the ending of the first person of the present indicative and perfect in *-c(h)* as in *mech.*

Linguistic analysis of the prayer and the other Old French texts in M729 reinforces the localization of the manuscript to the area of Picardy that included Soissons and Amiens.[78] Although the Picard dialect is incompletely known, and M729 offers too few examples for a secure analysis, it is possible to draw some tentative conclusions. The particular dialect characteristics may, of course, reflect the origins of the scribe rather than of the manuscript itself.

The province of Picardy contained three basically different, geographically defined trends in the formation of its general dialect. On the whole the Old French texts in M729 show phonological, morphological, and syntactic traits that most closely resemble those found in southwestern and central Picardy, especially at Amiens, Eu, Soissons, and Senlis. The characteristic forms of *orison, pisson,* and *sanler* appear at Amiens. The forms *Dieus* and *Mikieus* are frequent at Eu. The preference in M729 for *la* as the feminine definite article, *ma, ta,* and *sa* as the feminine possessive adjective, and *moi, toi,* and *soi* as the personal pronouns is typical of Soissons and Senlis. Eu and the southern towns prefer the verb form

78. The discussion of the dialect is based on Charles T. Gossen, *Grammaire de l'ancien picard* (Paris, 1970), the standard manual of the Picard dialect of Old French. For a more complete analysis of the Picard features in M729 see Gould, "The Psalter and Hours of Yolande of Soissons," pp. 62–66.

veoir and the nouns *diable* and *table*.[79] Together these traits offer at least partial confirmation of the other evidence regarding M729's origin.

A close look at various parts of the Psalter and Hours of Yolande of Soissons reveals significant facts about this manuscript's origins and historical context. The coats of arms suggest that M729 was made for Yolande of Soissons, the wife of Bernard V of Moreuil. Family history places the production of M729 in the last quarter of the thirteenth century, possibly around 1275 to 1285, and demonstrates that the Moreuil family was active and influential in an area located near Amiens. Textual analysis reinforces the importance of this geographical framework: the calendar emphasizes saints venerated at Amiens, while the dialect of the Old French texts also is characteristic of this region of Picardy. The manuscript itself thus provides a background for examining the stylistic and iconographic aspects of its decorative program.

79. For a list of characteristics used to localize the dialect in M729 and a table recording the results of this analysis see Gould, "The Psalter and Hours of Yolande of Soissons," pp. 67–71, 363.

II

THE ILLUMINATIONS

THE STYLE

The extensive and consistent decorative scheme that illustrates the Psalter and Hours of Yolande of Soissons is this manuscript's most notable feature. Full-page miniatures visually introduce the reader not only to the entire manuscript but also to the major textual divisions. Historiated initials and full-page borders that face the miniatures add emphasis to these sections. Within the larger units, the smaller decorated initials, curving branches of foliage, and patterned line endings that further separate and organize the text enhance almost every page with their bright colors and imaginative designs.

In the miniatures, the narrative scenes are placed inside two types of frames that combine architectural and purely decorative elements. In the most common of these two borders, piers, either painted to resemble brick or articulated with arches and niches, form the outer sides (figs. 1, 2). A flat band filled with heraldic motifs or decorative designs defines the bottom of the frame. Cusps terminating in heart- or trilobe-shaped finials surround the sides and bottom, while roundels are placed at the corners and mid-sides. A series of pointed arches supported by thin columns placed just inside each pier comprises the top of this frame. The resulting canopy combines trefoil arches surmounted by gables, lancet windows, pinnacles, spires, and flying buttresses into a painter's version of contemporary Gothic architecture.

The second border type appears only around the seven miniatures of the Psalter (figs. 10, 12, 14, 15, 16). Bands decorated with a foliate scroll replace the side piers and the architecture across the top, forming a uniform frame on all four sides. A simple architectural canopy remains beneath the upper band, although its supporting columns disappear. Cusps with trilobe finials continue to surround the sides and bottom, while the leaf finials of the architectural gables that overlap the top band provide a similar finish to this edge. There are also corner and side roundels.[1]

1. Only one miniature, Christ in Majesty (fol. 5r), lacks an architectural border. In

These framing devices are important both for their depiction of specific architectural structures and for their contribution to the development of the painted architectural border. Although the elements that comprise many of the architectural canopies in M729 seem to represent only general features of Gothic architecture, in several miniatures specific structural details as well as their particular configuration closely resemble parts of Amiens Cathedral.[2] The arches above the miniature of the Holy Face (fig. 7) provide one example of this relationship. The straight vertical openings of the upper part of the buttresses are a noticeable feature of the Amiens chevet (fig. 40).[3] Although in the miniature the arcaded buttresses lack the more complex combination of two lancets and a quatrefoil, they reflect the overall shape and disposition of this feature on the cathedral. Also, the inner buttress uprights in the miniature repeat the pattern of arches surmounted by pointed trilobes on the intermediate uprights of the Amiens choir buttresses. Although the illuminator simplified both the rendering of details and the complex relationships of forms in space, Amiens Cathedral provided a close visual source for the composition of this border in M729.[4] The cusped edges terminating in stylized leaf shapes that surround the bottom and sides of all the miniatures in M729 (fig. 4) may also reflect the inspiration of Amiens Cathedral. Similar cusps with tripartite leaf-shaped finials surround the lower edge of the portal arches on the west façade at Amiens (fig. 41).[5] These examples indicate that an artist who worked on the framing devices in M729 had carefully observed the architectural details of Amiens Cathedral.

---

this illumination, the narrow band that forms the quatrelobe frame for the figure of Christ also expands to surround the miniature. The cusped edges and heraldic roundels remain.

2. Carl F. Barnes, Jr., "The Architectural Motifs in the Psalter and Hours of Yolande of Soissons and the Cathedral of Notre-Dame at Amiens," *Gesta* 17/2 (1978), forthcoming, discusses many of the connections between the miniature borders and the cathedral architecture. I am indebted to Professor Barnes for providing me with a copy of this paper.

3. According to Robert Branner, *St. Louis and the Court Style in Gothic Architecture* (London, 1965), pp. 138–140, the construction on this portion of the chevet dates between 1258 and 1265. It was certainly completed by 1288 when the labyrinth inscription was placed in the nave. Barnes, "The Architectural Motifs," suggests that this form of buttressing began at Amiens.

4. Other miniatures in M729 employ variations on this depiction of the buttresses. See fols. 6v (fig. 4), 279v, 286v.

5. The west façade portals date from the earliest building campaign on the cathedral beginning around 1220. Branner, *St. Louis and the Court Style,* p. 138. Barnes, "The Architectural Motifs," discusses this feature in more detail.

These borders also demonstrate an advance in the spatial conception of the architectural border in French Gothic illumination.[6] In the St. Louis Psalter, one of the earliest examples of this style, an inner canopy of arches and an outer band decorated with leaf scrolls or gold tendrils make two separate framing devices (fig. 42). Although the M729 miniature borders reveal the inspiration of the St. Louis Psalter style in the repetition of decorative motifs and the similarity of the architectural members, both types of frames in the Yolande Psalter and Hours show an increased awareness of the three-dimensional illusion that these borders can create. In the M729 Psalter miniatures, the inner arches add a spatial dimension by overlapping the top band, but the pier borders show an even greater advance in spatial complexity. This type of frame not only eliminates the outer band at the top and sides but also gives a sense of receding space that leads into the miniature by placing columns just inside the piers. The miniature of Yolande in prayer (fig. 19) is particularly innovative because it attempts to integrate this architectural frame with an interior spatial setting, a technique not generally utilized until the fourteenth century.[7]

Inside the stage that these borders set, the tall, graceful figures are the focus of attention. Their usual costume is a tunic that falls in vertical, tubular folds with a mantle that drapes over one side of the body in V-shaped folds (figs. 12, 16, 25). Straight lines define the vertically falling drapery, and slightly curving lines with tiny hooks at the ends form the V-shaped folds. When these lines are applied over flat colors in the favored shades of red, blue and orange, they give only a slight indication of the movement of the body beneath, but often the drapery is modeled to show

6. For a discussion of the development of the architectural border see Karl Birkmeyer, "The Arch Motif in Early Netherlandish Painting," *Art Bulletin* 43 (1961), 5–9.

7. In the first half of the fourteenth century, Jean Pucelle, in miniatures such as the Annunciation in the Hours of Jeanne d'Evreux (New York, The Cloisters Collection, MS 54.1.2, fol. 16r), altered the traditional architectural frame into a building that simultaneously depicted both exterior and interior views. See Kathleen Morand, *Jean Pucelle* (Oxford, 1962), p. 15, pl. IXa, and Carl Nordenfalk, "Maître Honoré and Maître Pucelle," *Apollo* 79 (1964), 360–361. For miniatures that retain the more traditional form of architectural frame, Birkmeyer, "The Arch Motif," pp. 7–8, fig. 7, points to the dedication page of the Bible of Jean de Vaudetar (The Hague, Mus. Meermanno-Westreenianum, MS 10 B 23) illuminated by Jean Bondol in 1371, almost a hundred years later than the Psalter and Hours of Yolande of Soissons, as the initial step in connecting the architectural frame and an interior setting. Although in Bondol's miniature the tiled floor and conical canopy give a more convincing spatial appearance, both miniatures use basically the same techniques to describe an interior space.

highlights and shadows, producing the illusion of solid, three-dimensional figures.

This modeling is often applied to faces and nude bodies. In the Crucifixion scenes (figs. 3, 35, 36, 37), the modeling in light brown of arm and leg muscles, as well as the indication of the rib cage, gives the figure of Christ a volumetric quality. St. Francis's face (fig. 1b) shows a slightly wrinkled brow, and light brown modeling also defines the nostril. Even when the faces are painted in a flat ivory color, a delicate shading of orange along the jaw line adds color and roundness of form.

The faces display characteristic features. Two strokes define the eyes. The upper lid is rounded while the lower one varies from a slightly curved to an almost straight line (figs. 26, 33). A tiny line extends from the outer corner of each eye. Eyebrows are rounded or arched, and the nose line continues unbroken from one eyebrow. Noses are slightly pointed. The mouth consists of a downward turning line with a smaller line beneath. Women and unbearded men have rounding and at times receding chin lines (figs. 3, 21), while the chins of bearded men thrust out slightly. Black lines over a light wash of color delineate the strands of hair. Most men's hair styles have a short curling forelock with wavy shoulder-length hair brushing back from the face. Beards are short, and they part slightly in the middle. Women's heads are covered with kerchiefs or wimples.

Although the facial types are similar, individual expressions or features could be vividly portrayed as a scene required. The border figure of Goliath on the Beatus page (fig. 8) arches his eyebrows and grimaces in pain. Two men in striking profile eagerly await the distribution of food in the Miracle of the Loaves (fig. 14), and a soldier in the Massacre of the Innocents frowns menacingly as he carries out his task (fig. 29).

The narrative scenes take place within a shallow spatial setting. The figures stand out against flat backgrounds of either burnished gold or diapered patterns in red and blue. In outdoor scenes, a narrow brown band establishes a rocky ground line. A few trees with slender, curving trunks and bunched groups of leaves in green or blue add to the landscape effect. At times, clouds with undulating edges accented by graded strips of color are visible beneath the arches (figs. 2, 25).

Architectural settings, although less frequently used, are equally abbreviated. In the opening miniature, for example, the figures stand to the right of a gate with rounded brick towers on each side (fig. 1a). Like the trees, the structure is too small in proportion to the figures, and the border cuts it off from full view. In the most developed depiction of an interior scene (fig. 19), the artist relies on a floor that tilts upward, an arched door-way on the left, and an altar placed at a three-quarter angle to indicate the interior space.

Even within this shallow framework, the artist demonstrates an aware-ness of techniques for creating spatial effects. Whenever a group of figures is present in a scene such as the Death of the Virgin (fig. 30), the place-ment of figures in overlapping rows suggests a recession of planes. Cubic objects such as benches, tables, or altars are often depicted in a kind of two-point perspective (figs. 9, 12). The inconsistent use of these devices and the lack of proper proportional relationships, however, leave figures and objects isolated without the unifying space of a true landscape or interior setting.

The sixty-four historiated initials fill ten text lines.[8] They occupy only a portion of the text block, leaving some script on the right side. A red or blue diaper-patterned square edged in gold forms the background for the body of the initial, which is in a contrasting red or blue decorated with various designs that shade from lighter red or blue to white (figs. 9, 20, 28). The usual motifs are circles, a paisley design combined with scallops, a twisted rope pattern, a St. Andrew's cross motif, and an acanthus design. The background inside the initial is burnished gold.

In general the figure scenes in the initials have the same stylistic char-acteristics as the full-page miniatures. The facial types, with rounded eyes and downturned mouths, are identical with the larger figures. Treat-ment of the drapery folds and the combination of flat and modeled colors remain the same. Figures group together and overlap, and small trees or objects set the scene.

Some stylistic variations between the figural scenes in the historiated initials and those in the miniatures exist, however. In the initials, the fig-ures tend to be thinner, and at times their heads seem larger in proportion to the bodies (figs. 20, 22). Flat colors and an emphasis on line predomi-nate over modeled draperies. There are fewer figures within one scene, and there is a reduction in the number of accessory objects.

Two other types of initials are used in M729. Two-line initials are placed on a red or blue square whose corners are decorated with gold dots or white tendrils (figs. 11, 13, 32). The contrasting red or blue initial is

8. The thirty initials in the suffrages (fols. 253v–263v) are slightly smaller. They fill only six lines of text. The suffrage initials measure about 40 mm. × 38 mm. and the other historiated initials measure about 55 to 60 mm. × 55 to 60 mm.

usually decorated with white circles or other patterns found on the historiated initials. Foliate scrolls, interlaced animal designs, or small faces on a gold background fill the initial's interior. One-line initials are either blue with red flourishing or gold with blue flourishing. Line endings which alternate red, blue, and gold geometric patterns on the parchment ground add to the decorative scheme.

Borders completely surround the pages with historiated initials (figs. 12, 24). At the left side, the ends of the initial become leafy branches that form one or two roundels above and below the initial. Heraldic shields, faces, or a continued curve of the branch fill these areas. The branch then extends into bar borders that usually combine a narrow gold bar with red and blue bars decorated with a fine white scroll design. This bar frames the entire page. At the corners and mid-sides other leafy roundels or interlace patterns may be integrated into the border.

Partial borders decorate text pages with two-line initials. Either a branch curving from the initial's outer corners to form several scrolls with buds or leaves, or the tail of a beast beside the initial winds into the margin (figs. 11, 13, 32). The scrolls are placed on a background with cusped edges. The branches or bars terminate in a bud or a group of leaves.

Many figures, animals, and hybrid beasts inhabit the full-page borders, and single animals, birds, or grotesques often perch on the curving branches of the text pages. These marginal drolleries demonstrate the variety and invention in these popular decorative elements of Gothic manuscripts, especially in northern France and England.[9] Human figures play musical instruments, ride various kinds of animals, and joust. Dogs, rabbits, apes, and lions frequently appear, and owls and cranes are two of the many species of birds (figs. 8, 19). Hybrid forms, often with human heads and winged dragon bodies sit on top of the upper and lower bar borders (figs. 12, 17, 23). Most of the marginal figures are placed by themselves or in pairs to add a touch of humor or a decorative quality, but sometimes they show a more satiric intent. On folio 268 (fig. 24), a hybrid with a human head and a fish's body catches a fish with a fishing pole, and at the top of the page a young man crawls along the ground. A running dog bites his exposed buttocks while a hare stands to the side encouraging this chase of reversed roles by blowing a hunting horn. None of the figures or vignettes,

9. Lilian Randall, *Images in the Margins of Gothic Manuscripts* (Berkeley, 1966), pp. 3–9. For specific references to M729 see pp. 34, 66, 69, 72, 92, 95, 102, 106, 110, 121, 122, 124, 140, 146, 155, 166, 178, 198, 231, 235, fig. 383.

except for Goliath on the Beatus page, seems to have a specific meaning relating to the theme of the miniature or historiated initial.[10]

For a manuscript with such a full program of decoration, the illumination in the Psalter and Hours of Yolande of Soissons creates an impression of stylistic unity. The figures are well-proportioned and graceful. The use of line is fluid and economical, and the same straight and curving lines with the terminating hooks define the drapery. The drawing of facial features is consistent throughout the manuscript. The hairline extensions at the corners of the eyes and the downturned stroke for the mouth are two of the constant elements in the facial expression. A particular feature that occurs throughout both the miniatures and the historiated initials is a profile view of a man's face in which a slanting nose receives prominence (figs. 8, 14, 26, 27). Objects such as trees with their slender curving trunks and groups of leaves are also similar (figs. 1b, 2, 15, 25). Even many of the marginal figures display the characteristic facial definition, elegance of form, and use of modeling (fig. 22). In addition to these stylistic considerations, the skillful composition of illustrations reveals not only an awareness of the meaning and dramatic force of a scene but also the ability to order details of the events portrayed to produce the greatest visual impact.[11]

Although the illumination of M729 has been thought to be the product of one workshop, descriptions of the Psalter and Hours of Yolande of Soissons have suggested that two artists, possibly more, illuminated this manuscript. This separation of hands has been based primarily on variations in the amount of modeling of figures and drapery and on differences among facial expressions. These observations have not produced, however, a systematic division of the contribution of different illuminators.[12]

10. For the Beatus page see William D. Wixom, *Treasures from Medieval France* (Cleveland, 1967), p. 170.
11. See Chapter III, pp. 79, 103.
12. The catalogue entry from The Walters Art Gallery, *Illuminated Books of the Middle Ages and Renaissance* (Baltimore, 1949), p. 24, states that "several artists executed the miniatures, the most skillful employing a style resembling that ascribed to 'Maître Honoré' of Paris." In William D. Wixom, *Treasures from Medieval France*, p. 170, the entry for M729 says that "Two distinct hands have been observed in these miniatures. . . ." Although it is noted that both used common formats and decoration and were members of the same workshop, one of the artists "shows a greater interest in light and dark modeling of the faces, hands, and robes" and "gives greater diversity of expression to the physiognomies." The catalogue from The National Gallery of Canada, *Art and the Courts: France and England from 1259 to 1328*, 1 (Ottawa, 1972), pp. 86–87, reaffirms that "the manuscript was decorated by two artists, one of whom was the more talented," but also concludes that "the two artists were working in close cooperation."

Variations in quality do exist throughout M729. Some of the miniatures are the work of a gifted artist. The Creation of the Plants (fig. 25) is one example of this achievement. The figure of God the Father turns with a sweeping gesture to point to some trees on the right. The subtle and convincing modeling gives a fleshy quality to his face, neck, hands, and feet, while the softly modeled folds of his tunic and mantle add to the volumetric appearance. The delicate curves of the tree trunks and leaves as they bend in slightly toward the Creator show the artist's sensitivity to the ordering of the composition and his delight in rendering the plant forms. The decorative patterning of the leaves contrasts with the solidity of the figure, but the similarity of the curving lines unites all the pictorial elements. Many of the miniatures in the prefatory cycle and in the three offices of the Virgin, the Holy Spirit, and the Cross approach this standard of painting.

In contrast, other parts of the decorative scheme lack this inspired quality. In a miniature such as the Woman Taken into Adultery (fig. 16), the figures stand more awkwardly with legs slightly bent. There is less use of modeling, and the faces seem thinner and the features more pinched and compressed. Some of the miniatures in the Psalter cycle and many of the historiated initials display these characteristics as well.

Several hypotheses may explain these stylistic discrepancies. On the one hand, the variations may represent the stylistic changes and development of one artist. Alternately, several different artists working in individually distinguishable styles may have illuminated M729. A third possibility would attribute M729's decorative program to a workshop of closely associated artists. Except for stylistic considerations, M729 lacks any internal evidence to solve this problem. There are no signatures of scribes or illuminators, nor are there records of payment to any such craftsmen for their work on this manuscript. Since all the illumination is complete and forms an integral part of the manuscript's structure, no unfinished pages or miniatures provide clues about the artists' procedures.[13]

The extensive decorative program in the Psalter and Hours of Yolande of Soissons probably took a number of years to complete, and the illuminations offer some evidence of stylistic development. Some of the Psalter

13. See the collation, p. 1, n.1. In some cases the back of the miniature had no text written on it, and twenty of these miniatures were cut out of the manuscript. In other cases, the text continues on the back of the miniature, thus firmly establishing its place in the manuscript. The different length of text sections seems to have caused this varying treatment of a miniature's reverse side.

decoration, in particular, shows less realization of the potential for depicting forms in space than the remainder of the illustration. The borders of the full-page miniatures in this section lack columns supporting the arches, and flat decorative bands completely surround the miniatures (figs. 10, 12). At times, figures and objects are depicted as isolated entities (fig. 9). When groups of figures appear, often there is confusion in the placement and separation of hands and feet (figs. 15, 16). In contrast, in the miniature of the Death of the Virgin (fig. 35), the artist defined the heads more distinctly and presented the overlapping rows more clearly. Since the consistency of facial features, drapery modeling, and depictions of three-dimensional objects such as Lazarus's casket (fig. 12) unite the Psalter illumination with the entire decorative program, the stylistic limitations in this section may indicate an earlier stage of execution for this portion of the illustration.

Identifying and separating the contribution of individual illuminators is as difficult as determining stages of development within the illustration. At first glance, for example, the first two miniatures seem to exhibit quite different approaches to the treatment of figures and drapery (fig. 1). The modeling of St. Francis's body and habit gives the impression of a solid columnar figure, while the flat colors and linear drapery folds make the family group on the opposite page look less substantial. However, the similarity of the men's heads in both miniatures, the elegant and assured placement of the hands of both Yolande and her husband, and the sense of movement beneath the garment in the smallest boy's extended leg demonstrate that both miniatures share an awareness of form that could be the work of the same artist.

Even within single miniatures, the approach to the depiction of drapery changes. In the Nativity (fig. 21), both the handmaiden's brown tunic and Joseph's grey tunic and blue mantle fall in gently modeled folds. On the other hand, the Virgin's white tunic and her bed cover, in the same orange-lined blue as Joseph's mantle, are flat, with black outlines and fold lines. It thus appears that at least one illuminator of M729 used several interchangeable techniques to describe the drapery.

Variation in size among different parts of the illumination further complicates the problem. The more linear and less polished style appears more often in the historiated initials than in the miniatures. A comparison of the full-page miniature of the Noli me tangere from the prefactory cycle and an initial with this same subject at the suffrage to Mary Magdalen illustrates the difference that size of format played in the definition of form (figs. 4, 23).[14] In the miniature, the artist combined modeling, as seen in Mary's tunic and Christ's body, with the linear drapery folds of the voluminous mantles to produce solid, substantial figures. In the trees, the outlines are precise, and each leaf is individually painted and shaded. In the initial, a scene about a third the size of the miniature, all the colors are flat, and the bodies almost entirely lack modeling. The lines describing facial features and hair are more sketchy, and the quality of outline varies. The trees remain in the initial, but the leaves which are drawn over a single expanse of color are less clearly outlined. Although the basic composition, the linear delineation of drapery folds, and the definition of facial features are comprised of exactly the same elements, in the initial, forms are simplified and less precisely drawn. In the smaller format of the initial, a reliance on linear rendering was probably easier, and the necessity of fitting scenes into a smaller area might explain some of the awkward poses (figs. 22, 27).

Considering problems such as difference in scale and mixture of techniques, a precise separation of the contributions of various artists or a decision about the evolution of a single artist within the manuscript becomes a matter of speculation that overlooks the importance of the stylistic unity. If more than one artist illuminated M729, their styles mingle so closely that it is fruitless to divide them precisely. It is unlikely, however, that a single artist could have produced such an extensive scheme of illumination unaided, and a study of the decorative elements in M729 reveals some evidence of workshop practices. In several instances, compositions are repeated almost exactly. Two miniatures of the Crucifixion are similar except for the slight variations in the poses of Mary and John (figs. 3, 36). An even closer correspondence exists between the full-page Noli me tangere and the historiated initial of the same subject (figs. 4, 23). Certain figures are repeated in identical form. The singing cleric in the historiated initial on folio 123 appears again in the initial beginning the litany (figs. 17, 18), and the frontal head from the miniature of the Holy Face is repeated in the historiated initial depicting St. John (figs. 7, 34). Many of the animals in the borders are based on the same patterns. A favorite theme is the hound chasing the hare. The dog is sleek with a pointed muzzle and thin tail. This group, seen in profile, runs across the page numerous times in M729, going from left to right and also in the reverse direction

14. This full-page miniature measures 75 mm. X 119 mm. The initial measures 40 mm. X 38 mm.

(figs. 9, 18). A dog or rabbit often sits in the same pose in the text borders (figs. 11, 13, 32). The repetition of these compositions and motifs indicates that some standard designs, probably in the possession of a workshop, were used for some of the illustration.[15]

Although knowledge about actual workshop practices in the late medieval period is incomplete, evidence suggests that illuminators were specialists in particular parts of the illumination. For example, one artist might execute only "minor" decoration such as running titles, line endings, or ornamented initials. Other artists might be responsible for border designs.[16] Although it is impossible to determine an exact division of labor for the different decorative elements, it is probable that specialized artisans painted some of these parts of the illumination of M729. The slight variations in quality and style among miniatures, historiated initials, and borders that probably reflect the activity of more than one person are also best explained by the efforts of an *atelier* of well-trained illuminators whose work on this manuscript extended over a period of time long enough to encompass internal stylistic changes and developments. The total unity of style, however, indicates the presence of a skillful artist who closely guided the illumination of the entire manuscript.

RELATED MANUSCRIPTS

The richness and high quality of illumination make the Psalter and Hours of Yolande of Soissons an outstanding achievement in the art of the decorated manuscript that few manuscripts of this period can match. Because of the excellence of the Yolande Psalter and Hours, the impression has lingered that few manuscripts related to M729 have survived. There are, however, several manuscripts that, despite the lack of large modeled figures, closely parallel the drawing style, facial types, and

15. The use of common models or designs does not necessarily imply that the artists were working from a specific model book. The procedures, as suggested in Robert Branner, *Manuscript Painting in Paris during the Reign of St. Louis* (Berkeley, 1977), pp. 20–21, probably were based on the artistic training within an individual workshop where the illuminators learned the compositions of particular scenes with variants as part of the shop's repertoire.

16. François Avril, "Un Enlumineur ornemaniste Parisen de la première moitié du 14e siècle: Jacobus Mathey (Jacquet Maci?)," *Bulletin Monumental* 129 (1971), 249–257; Sonia Patterson, "Comparison of Minor Initial Decoration: A Possible Method of Showing the Place of Origin of Thirteenth-Century Manuscripts," *The Library*, ser. 5, 27 (1972), 23.

decorative motifs found in M729. These manuscripts represent important evidence for the localization of M729 and the artistic milieu in which it was created.

A Psalter and two Missals in the Bibliothèque Municipale at Amiens that were probably made for religious houses in or near Amiens display stylistic features similar to the Psalter and Hours of Yolande of Soissons. Of these three manuscripts, the decoration of the Missal, MS 157, is the most elaborate.[17] A large manuscript of 243 folios, it is written in a Gothic *textualis formata* in a single column of fourteen lines to a page.[18] Its decorative scheme consists of two full-page miniatures, twenty-two historiated initials, and numerous one- and two-line decorated initials.

Although the manuscript contains no later indications of provenance, the saints who have masses and whose names appear in the litany indicate that the Missal was made for Corbie. There are masses for Saints Peter and Paul, titular saints of the church at Corbie (fol. 5r);[19] Adalard, a prominent abbot at Corbie in the early ninth century (fol. 25r); Bathildis, the Merovingian queen who founded Corbie in the seventh century (fol. 26r, fig. 44);[20] and Saints Fuscien, Victoric, and Gentian, who were martyred at Amiens (fol. 18v). The litany includes Saints Anscharius (Anskar), a monk from Corbie who went to Scandinavia; Paschasius Radbertus, an abbot of Corbie; and Precordius, a monk at Corbie. Moreover, the coats of arms in the background of the miniature of the Coronation of the Virgin (fig. 46) combine elements of the heraldic device of the monastery of

---

17. M. Rigollot, *Essai historique sur les arts du dessin en Picardie*, Mémoires de la Société des Antiquaires de Picardie, 3 (Amiens, 1840), p. 383, pl. 22; *Catalogue général des manuscrits des bibliothèques publiques de France, Départements*, 19 (Paris, 1893), p. 70; Georg Vitzthum, *Die Pariser Miniaturmalerei von der Zeit des hl. Ludwig bis zu Philipp von Valois und ihr Verhältnis zur Malerei in Nordwesteuropa* (Leipzig, 1907), p. 155; Victor Leroquais, *Les Sacramentaires et les missels manuscrits des bibliothèques de France*, 2 (Paris, 1924), p. 178; Bibliothèque Nationale, *Les Manuscrits à peintures en France du 13e au 16e siècle* (Paris, 1955), p. 39; Bernard Gagnebin, "Le Livre d'heures d'Agnes de Savoie, comtesse de Genève," *Genava*, n.s., 11 (1963), 329, fig. 6; M. Alison Stones, "The Illustration of the French Prose 'Lancelot' in Flanders, Belgium, and Paris: 1250–1340,'" Ph.D. Dissertation (University of London, 1970), p. 263. The Bibliothèque Nationale catalogue dates this manuscript at the beginning of the fourteenth century.

18. The manuscript measures 205 mm. × 294 mm.

19. Pierre M. Heliot, *L'Abbaye de Corbie: Ses Eglises et ses batiments* (Louvain, 1957), p. 20.

20. Heliot, *L'Abbaye de Corbie*, p. 19; Patrice Cousin, "Les Origines et le premier développement de Corbie," *Corbie, abbaye royale. Volume du 13e centenaire* (Lille, 1963), pp. 19–22.

Corbie, confirming that the Missal was originally made for use at this monastery.[21]

A comparison of the two full-page miniatures in this Corbie Missal (figs. 45, 46) with miniatures in the Psalter and Hours of Yolande of Soissons reveals similarities in border design and figure style. The composition of the miniature frames that combine an outer band with an inner architectural canopy are almost identical in both manuscripts. In Amiens 157, the cusped edges with gold trilobe finials and the corner roundels filled with small figures recall the placement of similar elements in M729 (figs. 1, 10).[22] In addition, individual motifs in the Missal's frame find parallels in the Yolande Psalter and Hours. In Amiens 157, leaf scrolls trailing from the tails of facing pairs of hybrid beasts combined with four interlaced orange lozenges decorate the outer band of the miniatures' borders. Similar leaf scrolls fill M729's frames in the Psalter section (figs. 9, 10), while the paired hybrids and interlace patterns repeat throughout all the borders (figs. 17, 25, 34). As in M729, arches springing from thin side columns form a canopy over the figures. Both manuscripts utilize the trefoil arches, leaf crocketed gables, triple leaf finials, and intermediate spires to form this structure. In the Corbie Missal, however, unlike M729, all these architectural members are in gold outlined in black, and the arches never overlap the outer band.

The figure style of the two large miniatures in Amiens 157 is close to M729, as a comparison of the Crucifixion in the Missal with one of the Crucifixion scenes in M729 demonstrates (figs. 3, 45). In both the manuscripts, the monumental figures stand out against flat backgrounds. The Missal shows the contrast of sculpturally modeled drapery in Mary's and John's pink mantles with the flat color and linear drapery folds of their blue tunics. The modeling of Christ's body in light brown and the light orange shading along the jaw lines of all three figures match the techniques

21. The background is divided into lozenges. These lozenges alternate two heraldic devices: *azur, a fleur de lis or* and *or, an episcopal staff sable, two keys gules*. J. Meurgey, *Armorial de l'église de France* (Macon, 1938), p. 285, gives the following blazon for the coat of arms of Saint-Pierre de Corbie: "D'azur, à trois fleurs de lis d'or, à l'écusson d'or chargé de deux clefs de gueules passées en sautoir et d'une crosse de sable brochant sur les clefs et accompagnées en pointe d'un corbeau de sable passant sur le pied de la crosse, l'écusson timbré d'une couronne comtale." For variations of the coat of arms see P. Zurfluh, "L'Héraldique des abbés-comtes de Corbie," *Corbie, abbaye royale. Volume du 13e centenaire* (Lille, 1963), pp. 415–416.
22. The cusped edges are also a characteristic detail of the façade of Amiens Cathedral. See Chapter II, p. 26.

used in the M729 miniature. In both manuscripts, the fabric falls in the same curving V-shapes whose edges terminate with upturning hooks. The modeled draperies in Amiens 157 make less use of interior black lines to accent folds than the garments in the M729 Crucifixion, but the painterly drapery modeling is used in M729 as seen on the figure of the fool (fig. 12).

In Amiens 157, the faces are somewhat thinner and smaller in proportion to the body, but the facial features are similar to M729. The eyes share the corner extensions and the mouth turns down with the small line beneath. Details such as Christ's hair curling down his shoulder or the short curls turning back from John's face are alike in the two manuscripts. Despite basic resemblances among Crucifixion scenes in the later thirteenth century, the treatment of Christ's twisted legs and John's pose with one hand holding the book and the other palm turned out emphasize the close relationship between Amiens 157 and M729.

The style of the historiated initials is similar to the large miniatures. As in the Nativity (fig. 43), there is the same contrast of modeled and linear draperies. The characteristic facial features with corner lines at the eyes and downturned mouth continue. Several initials in the Yolande Psalter and Hours provide stylistic comparisons for the Missal's initials. The figure of David in an M729 initial (fig. 9) shows a similar treatment of the broadly modeled drapery. In the suffrage initial depicting the Noli me tangere (fig. 23), Christ's face has the same sunken cheeks, jutting chin, awkward delineation of the eyes, and exaggerated downward turning mouth line found on Joseph's face in Amiens 157. The curling lock of hair falling down Joseph's shoulder parallels Mary Magdalen's hair style in the M729 initial, while her rounded cheeks and curly hair are like the Virgin's face in the Nativity. The figures in the Corbie Missal, however, appear more slender and elongated, with smaller heads than their counterparts in M729.

The format and motifs of initials and border decoration are also similar in Amiens 157 and M729. The placement of the red or blue initials on a gold outlined square of a contrasting red or blue, the leaf scrolls or hybrid beasts at the left corners of each initial, the bars beside the text with white linear designs, and the curving branches ending with leaf sprays across the top or bottom of a page compare to elements of full-page and partial borders in the Psalter and Hours of Yolande of Soissons (figs. 13, 32, 43, 44). Individual motifs that decorate the initials repeat in both manuscripts. The interlace structure of the initial on folio 29r recalls the Beatus initial in M729 (figs. 8, 44). The seated lion with pointed mane, the crouching dog, and the seated rabbit are some of the animals that repeat patterns found in the M729 borders (figs. 13, 32, 43, 44). The five-lobed leaf with lighter shading in Amiens 157 (fig. 44) appears throughout the M729 borders (fig. 9).

The similarities between the Corbie Missal and the Psalter and Hours of Yolande of Soissons are strong. The figures in the large miniatures have the same monumental qualities. The drawing of facial features and drapery folds is similar, and both manuscripts combine modeled and flat colors in the rendering of the clothing. The decorative repertory of Amiens 157 and M729 employs the same patterns. The borders of full-page miniatures combine an outer band with an inner architectural canopy, and the curving leafy branches on the text pages are similar. The repetition of border animals such as the lion with its mane coming to a point above his head probably indicates the use of some common models. These resemblances justify the conclusion that Amiens 157 and M729 were illuminated in the same workshop.

A Psalter, Amiens MS 124, is a close stylistic relative of both M729 and Amiens 157.[23] The manuscript of 170 folios contains a calendar, the Psalter with canticles and litany, and miscellaneous prayers. The text in *textualis formata* is written on two columns, except for the calendar.[24]

The calendar (fols. 1r–6v) confirms that the manuscript was made for Amiens usage. On May 16, St. Honoré's name is recorded in blue, and his feast is designated "magnum duplex" with nine lessons. There is an octave on 22 May. St. Firmin, martyr and first bishop of Amiens, has four celebrations: his feast day on September 25 (name in blue, nine lessons) with an octave on October 2, the discovery of his relics on January 13 (in blue, nine lessons), the entry of St. Firmin into Amiens (three lessons and *Te Deum*) on October 10, and on October 16 the translation of his relics (nine lessons).[25] There is also a prayer requesting the intercession of St. Firmin (fol. 164r). The name of St. Firmin, confessor and third bishop of

23. Rigollot, *Essai historique*, pp. 111–115, 383–384, pls. 19, 23, 24; *Catalogue général*, 19:58–59; Vitzthum, *Die Pariser Miniaturmalerei*, p. 154; Günther Haseloff, *Die Psalterillustration im 13. Jahrhundert: Studien zur Geschichte der Buchmalerei in England, Frankreich und den Niederlanden* (Kiel, 1938), pp. 56–57; Victor Leroquais, *Les Psautiers manuscrits latins des bibliothèques publiques de France*, 1 (Macon, 1940–41), pp. 13–14; Stones, "The Illustration of the French Prose 'Lancelot'," pp. 263–264. Leroquais dates this Psalter mid-fourteenth century.

24. The manuscript measures 195 mm. × 294 mm.

25. Jules Corblet, *Hagiographie du diocèse d'Amiens*, 5 vols. (Paris, 1869–75), 2:46, 166, 172. The translation to a new gold *châsse* took place on October 16, 1204.

Amiens, appears in blue with nine lessons on his feast day, 1 September. The martyrs from Amiens, Fuscien, Victoric and Gentian, are written in blue on their feast day of December 11 (nine lessons). They are further honored with an octave on December 18 and the feast of the discovery of their relics with nine lessons on 27 June. St. Salvius, the bishop of Amiens who discovered the relics of St. Firmin I, is named on October 29 with nine lessons. December 17 commemorates the reception of the head of St. John the Baptist, which occurred at Amiens in 1206.[26] A later, probably fifteenth-century hand on folio 169v records, "Istud volumen est de ecclesia Sancti Martini ad Gemelos," and it is probable that this manuscript was made for use at Saint-Martin-aux-Jumeaux at Amiens.

This Psalter has six large historiated initials remaining at the ferial division of the Psalms.[27] The other Psalms begin with two- or four-line initials filled with leaf scrolls or interlace designs on a gold background. Red and blue bars that extend from most of these initials terminate in curving branches with leaves or buds. At times, animals or birds perch on the borders. Both the layout of the page and the ornamental details resemble M729 and Amiens 157 (figs. 13, 23, 43, 48). In addition, the calendar is illuminated with figures representing the occupations of the months beside the *KL* initials and roundels at the right side of the page with the signs of the zodiac (fig. 47). Numerous one-line initials with red or blue flourishing complete the decorative scheme.

A comparison of Beatus initials in Amiens 124 and M729 (figs. 8, 48) shows the stylistic relationships between the two manuscripts. In the upper loop of the *B* in Amiens 124, David plays a harp, and an organ rests beside him. In M729, David plays an organ, and, although the harping David of Amiens 124 is a more traditional representation in Beatus initials, the presence of the organ placed beside the figure in Amiens 124 may provide some connection with the more unusual depiction in M729. Although the poses differ, the figure style is much alike in the two manuscripts. In Amiens 124, David wears a grey mantle over a pink tunic whose curving folds are modeled. These colors are just the reverse of David's pink mantle and grey tunic, similarly modeled in M729 to give a plastic quality to the figure. In Amiens 124, David's face is slightly modeled, and the touches of

26. Corblet, *Hagiographie*, 5:65; Leroquais, *Les Psautiers*, 1:13.
27. The Psalter was originally illustrated with an eight-part ferial division. The initial for Psalm 26, *Dominus illuminatio* (fol. 28v), has been cut out, and the leaf containing Psalm 38, *Dixi custodiam* (fol. 42) has been removed.

orange along the line of his beard correspond to the facial coloring in M729. In the bottom half of the *B*, David's pose with his slingshot drawn back to one side and the rocky hill with sheep recall the setting of this scene in M729. The facial types are related, but the small heads and compressed features in Amiens 124 are even closer to Amiens 157 (fig. 45).

The composition of the initial is similar in Amiens 124 and M729. An interlace pattern forms the main structure, while the left corners become branches that form a circle around an heraldic shield. Amiens 124 elaborates the narrow gold border around the rectangle, with trilobe leaves sprouting from the outer edge and two additional coats of arms at the right corners.[28]

This comparison reveals the close stylistic resemblances among M729, Amiens 157, and Amiens 124. Parallels in both figure style and layout of these initials show their common artistic origins, and an exact correspondence in marginal details such as the lion, crouching dog, and rabbit that recur throughout these manuscripts (figs. 13, 32, 43, 44, 48) indicates that the artists were using similar models. The unity of style places this Psalter in the same workshop that produced M729 and Amiens 157.

A smaller Missal, also made for Corbie, Amiens MS 156, shows stylistic connections with this group of manuscripts, especially in its decorative motifs.[29] It consists of 395 folios written in *textualis* in two columns, except for the calendar (fols. 1r–6v).[30] The scribe gives his name, Girard of Amiens; the manuscript's date, 1289; and the person for whom it was made, Frater Johannes, on folio 272: "Frater Johannes de Candas tunc prepositus ecclesie Corbeiensis fecit fieri hoc missale. Anno Domini m.cc. octuagesimo nono. Per manum Girardi de Ambianis scriptoris. Orate pro eo." The calendar confirms that the Missal was used at Corbie. Saints of special importance indicated by red or blue script include Adalard (both his feast day and the elevation of his relics); Bathildis; the discovery of the bodies of Saints Fuscien, Victoric and Gentian; and the translation of relics of Saints Gentian and Precordius. Other Corbie saints in the calendar

---

28. The blazon for both coats of arms is: *gules, a bordure or, impaled with a lion and four bendlets of the same.* I have been unable to identify this heraldic device.
29. *Catalogue général,* 19:70; Vitzthum, *Die Pariser Miniaturmalerei,* p. 153; Leroquais, *Les Sacramentaires,* 2:165; Stones, "The Illustration of the French Prose 'Lancelot'," pp. 46, 224 n.3, 263–264.
30. The manuscript measures 142 mm. × 211 mm.

are Anscharius, Paschasius Radbertus, and Gerald, a monk at Corbie in the eleventh century.[31]

The decoration consists of seven historiated initials varying in size from six lines (fol. 21r) to nine lines (fol. 183v). Ten other large initials, from five to seven lines high, display leaf scrolls or interlace patterns on a gold ground. Partial curving borders appear on pages with historiated or large decorated initials. These bars have spiky cusped edges in red, blue, and gold, and often are accompanied by small animals such as the familiar dog and rabbit, or bird. (fig. 50).

The style of the historiated initials is similar, but less refined, than either M729, Amiens 157, or Amiens 124. In the Nativity (fig. 49), the figures are in exactly the same positions as in Amiens 157 (fig. 43), but all the colors in this initial are flat and transparent. Only the black lines indicate the drapery folds. The flat colors and linear structure recur in the other figural scenes, and the quality of the drawing is more abbreviated and angular than the flowing lines in M729, Amiens 157, and Amiens 124. While the facial features have characteristics similar to those in the other manuscripts, they are not as carefully delineated. The figural proportions, more stocky than those in Amiens 157, relate to M729 (fig. 22), as do the more lively gestures and facial expressions.

The similarities in figure style and the repetition of compositions such as that in the Nativity, however, connect Amiens 156 with the style of M729 and the other manuscripts. Examination of the decorative motifs confirms this relationship. The *I* of *In principio* (fig. 50) illustrates the use of decoration in Amiens 156. The initial fills the length of the left column. A beast with an orange head, blue body, and grey wings sits on top of the initial. His tail becomes a multicolored leaf scroll extending down the length of the gold shaft of the initial. Similar hybrids accompany initials in Amiens 157 and M729 (fig. 13), and the leaf scroll appears in M729 borders as well as in the outer band of Amiens 157's two miniatures (figs. 9, 45, 46). The bottom of the shaft ends in an interlace pattern that recalls similar interlace designs from the other three manuscripts (figs. 9, 43, 48). The leafy branch with a small bird on top also decorates text pages of these manuscripts.

While these parallels indicate the close community of style among Amiens 156 and the other manuscripts, the illumination of Amiens 156 is

31. The restoration and rebuilding of the church at Corbie in the Romanesque period was begun and directed by St. Gerald (or Gerard). See Heliot, *L'Abbaye de Corbie*, pp. 43–44.

less ambitious. There are no full-page miniatures, and the number of historiated and decorated initials is reduced. The figure style, although related to M729, Amiens 157, and Amiens 124, lacks the volume that the modeling in the other manuscripts produces, and the quality of line in Amiens 156 is less graceful. The script is also less formal. The basic stylistic characteristics associate Amiens 156 with this workshop, but not with the production of the most accomplished artists.

These three manuscripts, Amiens 157, 156, and 124, not only form a stylistic group but also provide evidence for localizing their place of production. One of the manuscripts, Amiens 156, contains a scribal signature of Girard of Amiens and names a monk at Corbie, Frater Johannes, as the person for whom the manuscript was made. Saints in the litany and masses as well as a coat of arms show that Amiens 157 was also made for Corbie, and to judge from its calendar and later inscription, Amiens 124 was made for use at Amiens, possibly at Saint-Martin-aux-Jumeaux. Although scribes might move from place to place and a religious house could commission a manuscript from any scriptorium or illuminator's *atelier,* the conjunction of a scribe from Amiens, two manuscripts made for Corbie, and one manuscript of Amiens usage suggests that Amiens was the location of the workshop that decorated these stylistically unified manuscripts.[32] Stylistic parallels with M729 confirm other evidence from the saints in the calendar, architectural motifs in the borders, and iconography of certain miniatures of an Amiens localization for the Psalter and Hours of Yolande of Soissons.[33]

Stylistic analysis can connect other less securely localized manuscripts with this Amiens group. One such manuscript is a Psalter in the Pierpont

---

32. Since two of the manuscripts were made for Corbie, the question could arise whether the group of illuminators were connected with a monastic scriptorium there. This assumption is unlikely for several reasons. The lay status of the scribe as indicated by his signature points to a group of artisans working in the lay community. In addition, by this period, the once flourishing scriptorium at Corbie was no longer active, and the abbey was acquiring books by donation. The same Frater Johannes who commissioned the Missal, Amiens 156, for example, also ordered or bought other manuscripts for the church and abbey at Corbie. See Leopold Delisle, "Recherches sur l'ancienne bibliothèque de Corbie," *Bibliothèque de l'Ecole des Chartes* 21 (1860), 420. Johannes de Candas gave "pro obitu suo" two Missals for the main altar and two Missals for the chapel of St. Lucien. He also purchased in Paris on January 27, 1297, a copy of the *Summa* by Raimond de Pennaforte (now Amiens, Bibliothèque Municipale, MS 267). Perhaps the Missal, Amiens 157, is part of his donation.

33. See pp. 14–18, 26, 108–115.

Morgan Library, M796.[34] The manuscript of 153 folios is written in *textualis formata* in double columns.[35] It contains the Psalter with canticles and litany, but lacks a calendar. Saints in the litany emphasize northern France, and some point particularly to the area of Amiens.[36] The heraldic shields, though difficult to identify with certainty, also point to the Picard region.[37] The inclusion of St. Louis in the litany (fol. 150v) suggests a date after his canonization in 1297 for this manuscript.

The illumination consists of eight large historiated initials at the ferial divisions of the Psalter. Full borders surround the pages with these initials. Two-line decorated initials begin the other Psalms. Branches with leaves or buds extend from the left corners of these initials to form a partial border that curves across the top and bottom of the page. The curving ends terminate with leaf sprays, and animals and birds perch on these branches. One-line initials of gold, red, and blue with red and blue flourishing begin the verses of the Psalms. There are decorated line endings in the litany.

34. Hans W. Janson, "A 'memento mori' among Early Italian Prints," *Journal of the Warburg and Courtauld Institutes* 3 (1939–40), 245, pl. 376; Randall, *Images in the Margins*, pp. 62, 68, 73, 75, 92, 120, 125, 140, 142, 145, 146, 154, 168, 216, 217, 218, 226, 230; John Plummer, *Liturgical Manuscripts for the Mass and the Divine Office* (New York, 1964), p. 38, pl. 17. Plummer dates the manuscript at the end of the thirteenth century and suggests that it may have belonged to the Abbey of St. Fuscian at Amiens.
35. The manuscript measures 240 mm. × 334 mm.
36. Saints Firmin I, Fuscien, Victoric, and Gentian are listed among the martyrs (fol. 150v), and Saints Firmin II, Honoré, and Salvius are recorded with the confessors (fol. 150v).
37. Four different heraldic devices are found in the borders. On fol. 1r in the lower right corner are two shields with *barruly argent and gules* and *gules, a cross or.* The jousting knights on the bottom of fol. 75v have the same coats of arms except that the *barruly argent and gules* adds *a bend gules.* The tinctures of these two devices are repeated on the garments of a man and lady in the border of fol. 106v. A possible identification for the device, *gules, a cross or* is the Varennes (or Warennes) family. See Théodore de Renesse, *Dictionnaire des figures héraldiques*, 5 (Brussels, 1903), p. 45. For this Picard family see Anselme de Saint-Marie, *Histoire généalogique et chronologique de la maison royale de France . . . ,* 9 vols., 3rd ed. (Paris, 1726–33; repr., Paris, 1967), 6:637–639. Another possibility is to associate the *barruly argent and gules* with the Los family, seigneurs of Agimont (Renesse, *Dictionnaire*, 5:642, and Anselme, *Histoire généalogique*, 2:334). Jean de Los, seigneur of Agimont (d. 1310), was married to Marguerite of Nesle, daughter of Jean IV (or II) of Nesle, seigneur of Falvy and de la Herelle. According to Renesse, *Dictionnaire*, 5:45, the device *gules, a cross or* can also be associated with the Nesle (or Neelle) family. A grotesque in the upper left border of fol. 75v has a shield with the device, *gules, a lion rampant or.* In the bottom border of fol. 90v is the coat of arms, *gules, a band or with a label azure.* I have not been able to identify these coats of arms satisfactorily.

A comparison of Beatus initials in M796, M729, and Amiens 124 shows the parallels in figure style and decorative motifs and demonstrates the combinations and reworking of these stylistic elements within a workshop tradition (figs. 8, 48, 51). All three initials share the same interlace structure and figural scenes of David as a musician in the upper loop of the *B*, with David and Goliath below. The choice of David playing an organ for the upper illustration in M796 provides an iconographic connection with M729. In the Yolande Psalter and Hours, David occupies a more central and unusual position, but the figure behind the organ is similar. The colors of the garments that David wears, pink and grey for mantles and tunics, are alike in both manuscripts, and the modeled drapery falling in soft folds is also similar. The M796 Beatus initial, however, resembles the initial in Amiens 124 even more closely. The interlace structure that is set more rigidly into the initial's framework is almost identical. The lower scene of David and Goliath repeats exact elements such as the expression on Goliath's face and the small dog, with positions reversed, between the two figures. David's placement, his pose, and the drape of the mantle in the upper part of the M796 initial compare with the harping David in Amiens 124. In M796, David's upraised hand may derive from a model of David playing a harp, as in Amiens 124. In addition to these compositional similarities, the figure style, especially the drawing of facial features, is close enough to suggest that the same artist was responsible for both of these initials. While these three initials share structural, stylistic, and thematic relationships, the M729 artist presented these elements in the most inventive way. The Beatus initials in M796 and Amiens 124, while attaining a high quality of visual presentation, lack the creative vision found in M729.

All of the historiated initials in M796 display the same figure style, which is characterized by slender, upright figures wearing garments with modeled drapery accented with black lines (figs. 52, 53), but the border figures do not have this elegance. On the Beatus page, for example (fig. 51), the musicians in the roundels beside the initial and in the right border medallions have large heads in proportion to their bodies. The drawing of facial features is less refined, and the drapery is flatter and more linear. These characteristics are not unique to M796, and comparisons for these stylistic features appear in the calendar illustrations of Amiens 124 and to some extent in M729 (figs. 5, 47).

Initials and borders also relate to the Amiens manuscripts, but there are differences. The wide portions of the eight large initials consist of interlace alone. While the Beatus initials in M729 and Amiens 124 (figs. 8, 48) have the interlace structure, a majority of the initials in these Amiens manuscripts are red or blue with white designs on the body of the initial. Leaf scrolls beside the initials and at the corners, red and blue bars with white geometric or scroll patterns, and leafy branches compose the borders in M796 as in the other manuscripts, but M796 mixes these motifs in new ways, as can be seen on folio 75v (fig. 52). Examples of these variations in border motifs are evident in the gold trilobe leaves that sprout from the narrow gold band of the left bar and the repetition of interlaced lozenges with interspersed leaves across the lower border. Similar trilobe leaves surrounded the Beatus initial's frame in Amiens 124, and isolated interlace patterns were used in the borders of M729 and Amiens 157 (figs. 34, 45), but their particular elaboration and arrangement is different in M796. Marginal drolleries such as the jousting knights, the dog chasing the hare, and the owl (figs. 51, 52) are very close to similar subjects in M729 and the related manuscripts (figs. 19, 27, 44), but in M796 these figures are smaller, and the outlines are darker.

Many aspects of the illumination in M796 resemble the Amiens group. Figure style, facial features, and subjects are comparable. Decoration in initials and borders repeats motifs found in the Amiens manuscripts. These stylistic similarities, in addition to the Amiens saints in the litany and the possible Picard character of the coats of arms, associate this Psalter with this Amiens group.

Another Psalter in the Bibliothèque Nationale, lat. 10435, is a richly illuminated manuscript that is connected stylistically with these Amiens manuscripts.[38] The text of 186 folios consists only of the Psalter with canticles, written in a single column of eighteen lines in a *textualis* script.[39] Since the manuscript lacks a calendar or litany, a positive localization is difficult. However, the dialect of the French rubrics that accompany and

---

38. Leopold Delisle, "Livres d'images," *Histoire littéraire de la France,* 31 (Paris, 1893), pp. 279–280; Samuel Berger, "Les Manuels pour l'illustration du psautier," *Mémoires de la Société nationale des Antiquaires de France* 68 (1898), 124–134; Vitzthum, *Die Pariser Miniaturmalerei,* pp. 153, 156–159; Haseloff, *Die Psalterillustration,* pp. 34–39, 56–57, 116–117, pl. XV; Leroquais, *Les Psautiers,* 2:95–98; Bibliothèque Nationale, *Les Manuscrits à peintures,* pp. 35–36; Stones, "The Illustration of the French Prose 'Lancelot'," pp. 263–265. Leroquais dates the manuscript in the second half or at the end of the thirteenth century. The Bibliothèque Nationale catalogue dates this Psalter around 1290.

39. The manuscript measures 125 mm. × 180 mm.

explain the illustration of many of the Psalms is Picard.[40] The line endings contain numerous heraldic shields, and in some of the borders the figures are named. Although the connection of many of the blazons and names with historical persons is problematic, the identifiable figures are from the Picard region.[41] This evidence supports several scholars' localization of lat. 10435 at Amiens.[42]

The program of decoration is extensive. Eight large historiated initials occupying between ten and fourteen text lines mark the ferial division of the Psalter. With one exception, these initials contain two separate scenes. One sequence illustrates the text of the appropriate Psalm with scenes from David's life or the standard system of word illustration, while the other series depicts the Creation.[43] Smaller historiated initials, approximately three lines high, begin each of the remaining Psalms. These initials are in red or blue with the lighter shaded circles, St. Andrew's cross, and twisted rope designs. Contrasting red or blue squares decorated with white tendrils and gold dots surround the initials, and the interior background is burnished gold. The varied subjects of these scenes also are based on a type of word illustration.[44] One line initials begin each verse of the Psalms. The initials are in burnished gold and are placed on a pink or blue square that is outlined in black and filled in with delicate white ornamental patterns. Rectangular line endings usually decorated with heraldic shields and hybrid beasts fill out spaces in the text. A rectangular bar border surrounds almost every page, and numerous animals, birds, human figures, and grotesques combined with foliage enrich these borders.

This Psalter presents a compendium of stylistic and iconographic motifs found in the M729 group of manuscripts although it also displays some original features. A comparison of lat. 10435 and M729 demonstrates

40. Berger, "Les Manuels," pp. 128–134, publishes these notes. For their Picard character see Leroquais, Les Psautiers, 2:96; Bibliothèque Nationale, Les Manuscrits à peintures, p. 36.
41. Some of the names are mentioned in Delisle, "Livres d'images," p. 280, and in Leroquais, Les Psautiers, 2:95–96. The catalogue from the Bibliothèque Nationale, Les Manuscrits à peintures, p. 36, identifies many of the names and suggests that the names were written in by one of the original owners.
42. Vitzthum, Die Pariser Miniaturmalerei, p. 153, and Haseloff, Die Psalterillustration, p. 56, suggest a localization at Amiens-Corbie for this Psalter. Stones, "The Illustration of the French Prose 'Lancelot'," pp. 263–265, mentions this manuscript in connection with other Amiens manuscripts.
43. See Haseloff, Die Psalterillustration, pp. 56–57, 116–117, for these subjects.
44. For a list of subjects see Leroquais, Les Psautiers, 2:96–98.

their similarities. These two manuscripts are the only members of this group that share a page layout with rectangular bar borders (figs. 27, 54). The combination of gold bands and blue or pink bands with fine white patterning is identical, as is the composition of the border frame with leaf scrolls and curving extensions surrounded by cusped edges at the corners and interlace motifs interrupting the bars at regular intervals. Lat. 10435 varies this structure slightly by consistently placing the thin band in the middle of the bar and accenting the corners with the triple curving extensions. Other parts of the decorative scheme also appear in M729. Border scenes such as the jousting knights and some of the individual animals and grotesques are repeated in both manuscripts (figs. 19, 27, 54). The line ending on the first folio of the Psalter depicting a beast with a single, frontally placed head from which two profile bodies emerge on either side compares with similar decorative hybrids in M729 (figs. 4, 54). The choice of iconography and the composition of these scenes form other important links with the Psalter and Hours of Yolande of Soissons. Both manuscripts, for example, feature Creation cycles in unusual relationships to the text, and the compositions for the individual days are alike.[45] The program in lat. 10435 of illuminating each Psalm with a kind of word illustration is used, to a more limited extent, in M729.[46]

Although the figure style in the large initials of lat. 10435 repeats the characteristic type found in the Psalter and Hours of Yolande of Soissons, the figures lack M729's refinement. The Missal, Amiens 156, provides closer stylistic parallels (figs. 49, 54). In both of these manuscripts, the outlines tend to be darker and irregular in width. The lines describing drapery folds and facial features have a sketchy quality, and they are at times straight and angular, as seen on the Virgin's tunic in Amiens 156 and Goliath's surcoat in lat. 10435. The faces appear more plump, and the women's chins are rounded. The outer extensions from the corner of the eyes are prominent, and the mouth line sometimes turns upward slightly, as on the women's faces. The figural proportions with larger heads, the spontaneous quality of the drawing, and the gestures combine to give the

---

45. The Creation cycle in M729 illustrates the Hours of the Holy Spirit. For the subjects see Table 3. In lat. 10435, the subjects are similar to M729 except for the addition of the Creation of Adam (fol. 98v) as a scene separate from the Creation of Eve (fol. 117r), and the Creation of the Fish (fol. 61v) separate from the Creation of the Animals (fol. 78r).

46. The full-page miniatures that illustrate the Psalter in M729 depict New Testament scenes. The choice of these subjects is related to the particular Psalm because it recalls words or verses from that Psalm. See pp. 69–70.

figures an alert, lively appearance. These resemblances suggest that the same artist may have executed the large historiated initials in these two manuscripts.

Other stylistic elements in lat. 10435 appear in the other two Psalters, Amiens 124 and M796. In these three manuscripts, the interlace structure set into the initial is almost identical (figs. 48, 51, 54). The figures that occupy the smaller historiated initials in lat. 10435 (fig. 55) find stylistic companions in Amiens 124 in the calendar illustrations (fig. 47) and in M796 in some of the borders (fig. 51). All of these figures share the large heads and hands, the heavy outlines, the cruder definition of facial features, the more angular and scratchy drapery lines, and the awkward poses. In all these instances, the small formats help to explain the limited stylistic finesse in comparison with the other illumination. The elaboration of some border motifs such as the interlaced lozenges is also similar in lat. 10435 and M796 (figs. 52, 54). Thus, despite the distinct features in lat. 10435 such as the solidly painted rectangular line endings and one-line initials, the numerous resemblances to many aspects of this Amiens style place this Psalter within this group.

A copy of a didactic treatise in French, the *Livre de Sidrach* (Bibliothèque Nationale, fr. 1159), has no internal evidence for localization or dating, but relates in style to these Amiens manuscripts.[47] This volume contains 170 folios, but the end of the text is missing.[48] There are ten miniatures, but the first one is in a later style. There are numerous one- and two-line initials in red and blue decorated with penwork flourishing. Larger painted initials begin the sections illustrated by miniatures (fig. 56).

The scene of Noah directing the animals into the ark (fig. 56) shows the similarities to figural scenes in the Amiens manuscripts. Most of the colors are flat, and lines describe the figures and drapery folds. The tall figures resemble those of the Amiens style, as do the features and orange shading on the faces. The plants with the tightly grouped but individually drawn leaves are close to landscape details in M729 (figs. 1b, 25, 56).

47. This book in which Sidrach revealed the nature of the Trinity and answered innumerable questions for a heathen king, Boctus, was written either around 1243 or later in the thirteenth century. For a general discussion of this work see Ernest Renan and Gaston Paris, "La Fontaine de toutes sciences du philosophe Sidrach," *Histoire littéraire de la France*, 31 (Paris, 1893), pp. 285–318; Charles Victor Langlois, *La Connaissance de la nature et du monde au Moyen Age* (Paris, 1911), pp. 180–264. Langlois mentions fr. 1159 on page 201. I would like to thank M. François Avril for calling this manuscript to my attention.
48. The manuscript measures 205 mm. X 270 mm.

The partial borders that begin beside the decorated initials also relate to the style of this Amiens group. On folio 59v (fig. 56), for example, the initial forms interlaced branches at the bottom of the page and then curves into branches across the lower margin. The fanciful hybrids and lion are typical of the animals that occupy the borders. Similar beasts and curving branches also decorate manuscripts in the Amiens group (figs. 13, 43, 48, 56). These similarities in figure style, linear technique, and ornamented borders associate fr. 1159 with the Amiens manuscripts. The predominant use of flat colors and heavy outlines places the Sidrach manuscript especially close to Amiens 156 (figs. 49, 56) and suggests that fr. 1159 is a workshop production of this group.

While similarities in color, figure style, facial features, and handling of drapery, as well as formats and details of initials and border ornament, unite these manuscripts, variations in style and quality make it possible to establish more precise relationships of manuscripts within this group and to identify the contributions of some individual artists. The extensive program of decoration and its high quality set the illumination in the Psalter and Hours of Yolande of Soissons apart as the most outstanding manuscript in this group. The interplay of subtle modeling of tones with clear, bright colors and fluid lines produces an emphasis on substantial but graceful figures accented by richly designed foliage ornament. A creative approach to compositional arrangement is another important aspect of this manuscript's stylistic achievement. As on the Beatus page (fig. 8), the seated David's position on the bar of the initial and the expansion of the spatial continuum into the border for the David and Goliath scene demonstrate the imaginative use of the manuscript's format to enhance the visual potential of a scene.

The Missal, Amiens 157, and the two Psalters, Amiens 124 and M796, form a unified group that reproduces stylistic elements found in the Psalter and Hours of Yolande of Soissons at a high level of quality but without M729's characteristic verve. Both figure style and treatment of border ornament connect these three manuscripts. The figures tend to be slender, and their small heads add to the impression of elongated proportions (figs. 46, 48, 53). The facial features are precisely drawn, and the almond-shaped eyes, pointed noses, and thin mouths give a pinched look to the expressions (figs. 46, 48, 51). The drapery, often articulated by modeling alone, is heavy and falls in groups of multiple folds, as on the mantles of seated figures in Amiens 157 and M796 (figs. 46, 53). The border decoration shares the repetition of exact forms of animals and birds (figs. 44, 48, 52) and the closely spaced leaves branching symmetrically from the curved stems. These similarities indicate that some of the same illuminators decorated Amiens 157, Amiens 124, and M796, and it is probable that one artist was responsible for the historiated initials in Amiens 124 and M796.

A comparison of these three manuscripts with M729 shows that while the basic features of the M729 style remain, the Missal and two Psalters vary these stylistic elements. The figural proportions are adjusted to produce more elongated figures with smaller heads and hands. Drapery modeling is often increased, with less use made of interior black fold lines, but this change produces voluminous garments that hide the figure in an interplay of folds that have little organic connection with the body (figs. 46, 53). The facial features are smaller, thinner, and more tightly drawn, and the expressions lack the variety and spontaneity found in M729 (figs. 45, 48, 51). In the border decoration, animals and leaves are smaller in relation to the marginal space, and the symmetrical outgrowth of leaves contrasts with the natural exuberance of M729's borders (figs. 8, 12, 44, 52).

The other Corbie Missal, Amiens 156, and the *Livre de Sidrach*, fr. 1159, also share the basic stylistic features, but their decoration lacks refinement in painting and drawing techniques. In both these manuscripts, heads, hands, and feet often are large in proportion to the size of the body (figs. 49, 56). Flat colors predominate over the use of modeling, and heavy black lines outline the figures. The drawing of facial features is more irregular, and the eyes are often large and rounded. The border ornament is thicker, with heavier outlines. The cusped edges are more widely spaced, and the forms and outlines of leaves are simplified. These correspondences are close enough to conclude that some of the same artists worked on both of these manuscripts. Although this Missal and the *Livre de Sidrach* do not reach the level of quality found in the other manuscripts, the drawing style and gestures capture a feeling of lively activity characteristic of the illumination in M729 but rarely present in the other subgroup.

The remaining manuscript, B.N. lat. 10435, represents a unique combination of stylistic elements found in these Amiens manuscripts. The figure style of the eight large historiated initials, the heavier outlines, the broader spacing of the decorative cusping, and the less precisely articulated leaf forms place this Psalter's stylistic execution closest to the Amiens 156 Missal and the *Livre de Sidrach* (figs. 49, 54, 56). The script in lat. 10435 and Amiens 156 is also almost identical. However, this manuscript shares several important features with M729. Both manuscripts frame pages with rectangular bar borders enlivened by leaf scrolls, curving extensions, inter-laced lozenges, and numerous marginal figures. The ambitious iconographic programs in these two manuscripts have similarities in the selection of some subjects and in the relationship of illustration to text. From the sub-group of Amiens 157, Amiens 124, and M796, this Psalter repeats the interlace structure of initials, the stockier figure type of the small initials, and the elaboration of certain border motifs. The entire decorative pro-gram in lat. 10435 demonstrates how illuminators of differing talents but united by a common training within a workshop could combine their efforts to fill every page of a manuscript with illumination.

Although few of these manuscripts contain specific indications for dating, an examination of the available evidence helps to clarify the date of the Psalter and Hours of Yolande of Soissons and to establish a chrono-logical framework for this stylistic group. The only manuscript that is dated, Amiens 156, was written in 1289 according to the scribal colophon. The inclusion of St. Louis in the litany places M796 after 1297. Except for M729, none of the other manuscripts can be dated more precisely.[49]

The historical situation of Yolande of Soissons and her family pro-vides some evidence for dating M729, but this documentation is inconclu-sive. In particular, the birth dates of Yolande's children can only be approximated, and the use of this information to date the miniature depicting Yolande and her husband with two of their sons produces a probable range of about ten years, between 1275 and 1285, for the date of M729.[50] However, the other manuscripts in this Amiens group are dated later, from around 1290 into the early part of the fourteenth century, and the stylistic position of M729 suggests that it should not be separated chronologically from these manuscripts. Considering that M729 probably was illuminated over a period of time, a balance of historical and stylistic evidence weighs in favor of a date between 1280 and 1285 for the Psalter and Hours of Yolande of Soissons.

These dates set a broad chronological outline for the development of

49. A later manuscript that continues this style is a Missal now in The Hague, Bibli-othèque Royale, MS 78 D 40, which is dated 1323. The manuscript was copied by Garnerius of Moreuil and illuminated by Petrus of Raimbeaucourt for Frater Johannes de Marchello, abbot of Saint-Jean d'Amiens. See Vitzthum, *Die Pariser Miniaturmalerei*, pp. 153, 155; A. Byvanck, *Les Principaux Manuscrits à peintures de la Bibliothèque Royale des Pays-Bas et du Musée Meermanno-Westreenianum à la Haye* (Paris, 1924), pp. 19–22, pls. 7,8; G. I. Lieftinck, *Manuscrits datés conservés dans les Pays-Bas,* 2 vols. (Amsterdam, 1964), 1:41–42, 2:pl. 234.
50. See pp. 7–11.

this Amiens style. The Psalter and Hours of Yolande of Soissons, the earliest of the manuscripts under consideration, probably formed the stylistic source for these Amiens manuscripts. Its extensive decorative program, directed and largely executed by a gifted artist, provided a characteristic figure style and rich decorative repertoire that continued to be repeated and varied in an *atelier* that had produced M729. The Missal, Amiens 156, dated 1289, is an example of a slightly later and less polished version of the style in M729, and the stylistically related *Livre de Sidrach* probably dates in this period, around 1290 to 1300. Because of similarities in figure style with Amiens 156 and in page layout and iconography with M729, the Psalter B.N. lat. 10435, should also be dated around 1290. The closely united group of Amiens 157, Amiens 124, and M796 can be dated around 1300 or slightly later, judging from the *terminus post quem* of 1297 in M796. These three manuscripts retain a high standard of quality but reproduce stylistic features of M729 in a less inspired fashion that also indicates a later, more routine production. The tightening of the figure style combined with the elaboration of border motifs, particularly in M796, reinforces the idea of a workshop tradition that continued with alterations and modifications of style over a number of years in the late thirteenth and into the early fourteenth century.

It is evident from the consideration of this closely related group of six manuscripts that the Yolande Psalter and Hours was not an isolated stylistic phenomenon, but the progenitor of a distinct style that continued to be reproduced and varied in certain Amiens manuscripts in the period between the late 1280s and the early 1300s. Stylistic evidence therefore reinforces other internal evidence to place M729 in Amiens in the decade of the 1280s. Nevertheless, the stylistic group defined above speaks only to the fate of the style of M729, and not to its artistic sources. A wider perspective is required to clarify the antecedents of the Yolande Psalter and Hours, and the study must be expanded to include other styles of manuscript decoration produced at Amiens, as well as the stylistic trends in late-thirteenth-century Parisian illumination.

THE AMIENS STYLE AND PARISIAN ILLUMINATION

Scholars have long recognized that Amiens was a center of manuscript illumination in the late thirteenth century. Vitzthum grouped several manuscripts, including B.N. lat. 10435 and Amiens 124, 156, and 157 at Amiens or Corbie, taking the saints named in these manuscripts and the inscription in Amiens 156 as a basis for localization.[51] Haseloff, although considering only Psalter illustration, isolated a Picard group in which Amiens 124 and B.N. lat. 10435 were localized at Amiens-Corbie.[52] Loomis in his work on the illumination of the Arthurian legends pointed to an illuminated version of the complete Vulgate cycle now in the University Library at Bonn, MS 526, whose colophon states that the scribe, Arnulfus de Kayo, completed the manuscript in Amiens on August 27, 1286. Loomis tentatively assigned Bonn 526 and several other copies of Arthurian romance to a Picard school centered at Amiens.[53] Robert McGrath added other manuscripts to this Amiens group by comparing the miniatures in a copy of the romance of the Maccabees (Berlin, Deutsche Staatsbibliothek, MS Hamilton 363) with Bonn 526, and the illumination in a manuscript at Princeton (Garrett MS 125) with a Psalter assigned to Amiens in the Boisrouvray donation. He contends that Amiens was not only "the leading producer of Arthurian manuscripts from the period" but also a major center for the production of all types of secular manuscripts in France.[54]

Although the role of Amiens as a center of illumination would seem to be well established, several difficulties concerning the extent and influence of this school remain. One problem relates to the variations in style among manuscripts decorated in this leading French center for the production of secular manuscripts. Another unsolved question is that of the relationship between illuminators from Amiens and Paris in the second half of the thirteenth century.

A comparison of three manuscripts usually localized at Amiens illustrates the problem of stylistic diversity. In the complete Arthurian cycle,

51. Vitzthum, *Die Pariser Miniaturmalerei*, pp. 153–159.
52. Haseloff, *Die Psalterillustration*, p. 56.
53. Roger Sherman Loomis, *Arthurian Legends in Medieval Art* (London, 1938), pp. 94, 97. He gives the complete text of the Bonn 526 colophon: "Explicit. Arnulfus de Kayo scripsit istum librum, qui est ambianis. En lan del incarnation M. CCIIII ^{XX}VI el mois daoust le jour le s. iehan decolase. Ici fenist la mort dou roy Artu et des autres . . . Et tout le romans de Lancelot."
54. Robert McGrath, "The Romance of the Maccabees in Mediaeval Art and Literature," Ph.D. Dissertation (Princeton University, 1963), pp. 189–190, 196–197, 199; McGrath, "A Newly Discovered Illustrated Manuscript of Chrétien de Troyes' *Yvain* and *Lancelot* in the Princeton University Library," *Speculum* 38 (1963), 592. For the Psalter from Amiens in the Boisrouvray collection see Jean Porcher, *Manuscrits à peintures offerts à la Bibliothèque Nationale par le Comte Guy du Boisrouvray* (Paris, 1961), pp. 31–32, pl. IV, figs. 10–14.

Bonn 526 (fig. 57), the figures are short and stocky.[55] Drapery colors are flat, and the garments fall in simple folds that reveal little about the movement of the body. Prominent heavy black lines outline figures and objects, delineate drapery folds, and describe facial features. The faces, often rounded, usually have a smiling expression created by the upturned line of the mouth.

A volume containing two texts of the Arthurian cycle at the Bibliothèque Nationale, fr. 95, has also been assigned to Amiens.[56] The style in this manuscript is more elegant than the illuminations in Bonn 526 (figs. 58, 59). The figures are taller and more slender. The modeling of drapery and the graceful lines give the active figures a volumetric appearance. Faces tend to be rounded, and a little smile is a common expression. The fluid outlines give less prominence to linear qualities. Small curving bars ending in a bud and a cusped edge spiral out from the corners of the border in a characteristic whirling pattern.

The Psalter and Hours of Yolande of Soissons represents another aspect of the Amiens style. The fine, graceful lines and drapery modeling relate M729 to the style of fr. 95, but there are differences in the treatment of figures and border decoration. The faces in M729, while at times rounded, are more often somewhat rectangular, with a protruding chin. The mouth always turns down so that there is never the artificial smiling expression. The borders have few of the whirling extensions at the corners and use more naturalistic leaf branches to form corner roundels in the full borders and leaf sprays in the partial borders. The large, often modeled, figures in many of the full-page miniatures in M729 have no parallels in either Bonn 526 or fr. 95.

These three manuscripts illustrate three distinct styles, and yet the illumination of all three has been associated with Amiens at about the same date in the last quarter of the thirteenth century.[57] Two explana-

55. Ellen J. Beer, "Gotische Buchmalerei. Literatur von 1962 bis 1965 mit Nachträgen für die Jahre 1957 bis 1961," *Zeitschrift für Kunstgeschichte* 30 (1967), 83–85.

56. Loomis, *Arthurian Legends*, pp. 95–97, 114, figs. 224–236; McGrath, "A Newly Discovered Illustrated Manuscript," pp. 590–592; The National Gallery of Canada, *Art and the Courts*, 1:88.

57. Bonn 526 is dated 1286. Fr. 95 is dated around 1280 in the Bibliothèque Nationale, *Les Manuscrits à peintures*, p. 32; around 1290 in McGrath, "A Newly Discovered Illustrated Manuscript," p. 590; and in the last quarter of the thirteenth century in The National Gallery of Canada, *Art and the Courts*, 1:88. M729 can be dated ca. 1275–1285. See p. 52.

tions for this situation are possible. First, some of the manuscripts attributed to Amiens may have been produced elsewhere. Second, it is probable that several *ateliers* were illuminating manuscripts at Amiens at about the same time in distinctly recognizable styles.

Of the three manuscripts selected for stylistic comparison, the *Histoire du Graal*, fr. 95, has the least securely documented connection with Amiens since it contains no internal evidence for localization. Vitzthum recognized the difficulty in determining this manuscript's place of origin, and he localized it further north, at Maestricht.[58] Loomis, later supported by McGrath, preferred to associate fr. 95 with Amiens. The only basis for this localization, however, was the comparison with the signed and dated Arthurian cycle, Bonn 526, a manuscript which differs in style from fr. 95, reinforced by the supposition that Amiens was the major center for the production of secular, particularly Arthurian manuscripts.[59] These tenuous connections with Amiens indicate that the localization of fr. 95 remains an open question.

The stylistic differences between two manuscripts more securely localized at Amiens, Bonn 526 and M729, suggest that several illuminators were working in this city in the second half of the thirteenth century. Tax rolls show that numerous illuminators were active in Paris in this period, and it is possible that a similar situation existed in Amiens.[60] The citizens of this prominent cathedral city in Picardy must have had strong interests in literature and learning, as the case of Richard de Fournival demonstrates. A writer and chancellor of the cathedral chapter of Amiens (1241–1260), he had a library of perhaps 300 volumes, which, as he relates in the introduc-

---

58. Vitzthum, *Die Pariser Miniaturmalerei*, pp. 143–144. In the Bibliothèque Nationale catalogue, *Les Manuscrits à peintures*, p. 32, this manuscript is localized generally in northern France. M. Alison Stones, "Secular Manuscript Illumination in France," *Medieval Manuscripts and Textual Criticism* (Chapel Hill, 1976), pp. 87, 91–92, suggests a localization in the diocese of Thérouanne on the basis of liturgical and heraldic evidence in manuscripts stylistically related to fr. 95. For a summary of the problems relating to the localization of fr. 95 see Eleanor S. Greenhill, "A Fourteenth-Century Workshop of Manuscript Illuminators and Its Localization," *Zeitschrift für Kunstgeschichte* 40 (1977), 1–2.

59. Loomis, *Arthurian Legends*, p. 97; McGrath, "The Romance of the Maccabees," p. 199; McGrath, "A Newly Discovered Illustrated Manuscript," p. 593.

60. Robert Branner, "Manuscript-Makers in Mid-Thirteenth Century Paris," *Art Bulletin* 43 (1966), 65–67; Françoise Baron, "Enlumineurs, peintres, et sculpteurs Parisien des 13e et 14e siècles d'après les rôles de la taille," *Bulletin archéologique du Comité des travaux historiques et scientifiques*, n.s., 4 (1968), 37–121; Branner, *Manuscript Painting in Paris*, pp. 1–15, 156.

tion to his *Biblionomia,* was available to the citizens of Amiens.[61] Many of these books were copied for him, and their similarity in format and decoration makes them recognizable.[62] He may have relied on scribes and decorators available in Amiens to produce some of these manuscripts.[63] The monk from Corbie who commissioned the Missal (Amiens 156) and other manuscripts that were given to this abbey is another example of a person from the Amiens area who not only acquired manuscripts but also used the resources of the manuscript trade in this city.

An explanation of the stylistic diversity among illuminated manuscripts attributed to Amiens lies between these two possibilities. While more detailed study may reveal that some manuscripts now assigned to Amiens were made in other places, the existence of several *ateliers* within one city would account for some of these stylistic variations. It is clear that there was no single "Amiens" style in the late thirteenth century. The illumination of M729 and the group of manuscripts related to it represents one of several styles of manuscript illustration in Amiens, probably to be identified with the work of a single *atelier* in this center. The identification and separation of other Amiens workshops in this period, as well as an inquiry into the origin of their styles, awaits further investigation.

In many ways, the closest stylistic parallels for the decoration of the Psalter and Hours of Yolande of Soissons and the manuscripts related to it are found in manuscripts illuminated, not in Amiens, but in Paris in the second half of the thirteenth century. Particular similarities appear in works that have been connected with the Parisian illuminator Honoré, either as antecedents for his style—the Martyrology of Saint-Germain-des-Prés (Bibliothèque Nationale, lat. 12834)—or as examples of his early work

61. William M. Newman, *Le Personnel de la cathédrale d'Amiens (1066–1306)* (Paris, 1972), p. 37; Aleksander Birkenmajer, "La Bibliothèque de Richard de Fournival poète et erudit français du debut de 13e siècle et son sort ulterieur," *Etudes d'histoire, des sciences et de la philosophie du Moyen Age,* Studia Copernica, 1 (Krakow, 1970), pp. 117–210 (see especially p. 121 for the Introduction to the *Biblionomia*); Richard H. Rouse, "The Early Library of the Sorbonne," *Scriptorium* 21 (1967), 48–51.

62. Richard H. Rouse, "Manuscripts Belonging to Richard de Fournival," *Revue d'histoire des textes* 3 (1973), 254.

63. These manuscripts, dating from about 1230 to 1260, are earlier than the illuminated Amiens manuscripts of the last quarter of the thirteenth century. Manuscripts were probably written for Fournival in a number of places, and their localization is a complex question involving problems such as the transmission of texts and identification of exemplars. For some of these problems see Rouse, "Manuscripts Belonging to Richard de Fournival," pp. 254–255.

—the first folios of an Evangeliary generally associated with the Sainte Chapelle (British Library, Add. 17341).[64] A comparison of decorative features in these manuscripts and in M729 illustrates the stylistic resemblances. In figure style, both the Evangeliary and M729 employ a combination of modeled and flat colors, enhanced by clear, fine lines to define forms. The Evangeliary artist uses facial features which, as in M729, are characterized by the rounded eyes with lines extending from the outer corners and a downturned mouth with a dot just beneath this line (figs. 33, 61). The figures in the Martyrology display similar features, and the supple feeling for form defined by fine lines, as seen in the labor for July, closely compares to M729 (figs. 6, 60). Borders in Add. 17341 use the same components: red, blue, and gold bars decorated with fine linear designs in white; curving branches ending in leaves or buds; leaf scrolls with cusped backgrounds; and the familiar dogs, rabbits, and birds (fig. 62).

Although these manuscripts share many stylistic features, a close examination reveals important distinctions. The figures in the Evangeliary, as in the scenes illustrating Christ's entry into Jerusalem (fig. 61), are more slender, elongated, and erect than their counterparts in M729 (fig. 33). The faces are thinner and more rectangular. The small V-shaped line on the cheek that delineates the beard is a constant feature in Add. 17341 that is rarely present in M729. In the Martyrology, also, the lines are finer, and the angular folds are more sharply drawn (fig. 60). The approach to border design is different in the Evangeliary. As on folio 11, the decora-

---

64. For the Martyrology see Vitzthum, *Die Pariser Miniaturmalerei*, pp. 18–24; Bibliothèque Nationale, *Les Manuscrits à peintures*, pp. 19–20; Branner, *Manuscript Painting in Paris*, pp. 136, 239. For the Evangeliary see Vitzthum, *Die Pariser Miniaturmalerei*, pp. 32–39; The National Gallery of Canada, *Art and the Courts*, 1:76–77; Branner, *Manuscript Painting in Paris*, pp. 137, 239. Several scholars have found precedents for Honoré's style in the Martyrology. See D. H. Turner, "The Development of Maître Honoré," *The Eric George Millar Bequest of Manuscripts and Drawings, 1967* (London, 1968), p. 57; Larry M. Ayres, "The Miniatures of the Santa Barbara Bible: A Preliminary Report," *Soundings: Collections of the University Library* [University of California at Santa Barbara] 3 (1971), 7–8. Gerhard Schmidt, *Die Malerschule von St. Florian: Beiträge zur süddeutschen Malerei zu Ende des 13. und im 14. Jahrhundert* (Linz, 1962), p. 115, attributes these miniatures to Honoré himself. Scholars generally agree that, among several styles in Add. 17341, the first twelve folios represent the contribution of the best artist, and this illumination often has been assigned to the hand of Honoré. See Eric George Millar, *The Parisian Miniaturist Honoré* (London, 1959), p. 14; The National Gallery of Canada, *Art and the Courts*, 1:52; Gerhard Schmidt, "Materialien zur französischen Buchmalerei der Hochgotik I (Kanonistische Handschriften)," *Wiener Jahrbuch für Kunstgeschichte* 28 (1975), 163.

tive elements are precisely drawn and positioned (fig. 62). The elongated necks of the monsters on top of the initial intertwine in a controlled, symmetrical design, and the animals running across the bottom are frozen into static poses. In the M729 borders, in contrast, the branches curve in a more spontaneous and energetic manner, and the numerous animals and figures move more actively and freely (fig. 22).

Although the differences between the Parisian manuscripts and the Psalter and Hours of Yolande of Soissons show that they are not the work of the same artists or even of the same school of painting, their common stylistic vocabulary raises the question of possible influence between styles in Paris and Amiens. In a general way, Parisian illumination from the middle of the thirteenth century may have set examples for the decorative formats and figure style found both in Parisian and in northern French manuscripts. The architectural borders in M729 and Amiens 157 probably reflect an ultimate inspiration from the style of the St. Louis Psalter (fig. 42). Other ornamental motifs such as the trailing leaf scroll, at times emanating from the tails of dragon-like beasts, found in M729 and in Amiens 156 and 157 appear in the St. Louis Psalter and the Isabelle Psalter.[65] The use of clear, bright colors against gold, the definition of figures by supple lines, and the use of modeling to enhance the volumetric appearance of drapery folds also may derive from Parisian manuscripts beginning around 1250.[66] All of these stylistic characteristics may, however, represent general tendencies in Gothic illumination that were part of a stylistic development that embraced painting in manuscripts as well as works in other media.

65. Sydney C. Cockerell, *A Psalter and Hours Executed before 1270 for a Lady Connected with St. Louis, Probably His Sister Isabelle of France* . . . (London, 1905), pl. I; Branner, *Manuscript Painting in Paris*, pp. 132–136, 238–239.

66. Branner, *Manuscript Painting in Paris*, pp. 97–141. McGrath, "A Newly Discovered Illustrated Manuscript," p. 591, has pointed to Add. 17341 as a specific source for transmission of a Parisian style to Amiens by stating that Add. 17341 was "known to have been in the cathedral treasury at Amiens as early as the end of the thirteenth century. . . ." Add. 17341 was not, however, the manuscript that was at Amiens, but rather it was a Bible (Antwerp, Plantin Moretus Museum, MS 36), which according to Vitzthum was related to Add. 17341 in style. This Bible contains entries on fol. 497v from the cathedral of Amiens for the years 1285, 1287, and 1293, but these entries are in a later hand, so even this Bible may not have been in the possession of the cathedral treasury at Amiens at this period. See Vitzthum, *Die Pariser Miniaturmalerei*, p. 33; Greenhill, "A Fourteenth-Century Workshop," p. 23, n.3. At the present time, therefore, there is no direct evidence on the basis of these manuscripts for the transmission of a Parisian style to Amiens in the late thirteenth century.

On the other hand, it is equally possible, as many scholars have suggested, to see influence of northern French illumination on late-thirteenth-century Parisian illumination. The lively and robust nature of figure style and border ornament are qualities of northern French illumination that are said to have provided an invigorating stimulus for manuscript painting in Paris.[67] The Psalter and Hours of Yolande of Soissons has been cited as one possible source for a late-thirteenth-century Parisian style, particularly seen in manuscripts associated with the illuminator Honoré. The three-dimensional appearance of figures in M729 with the skillful modeling of drapery folds has been seen as a precedent for the figures in such works as the frontispiece of the Breviary of Philippe le Bel (Bibliothèque Nationale, lat. 1023).[68] The discovery that Honoré's name was recorded in Parisian tax rolls as "Honoré d'Amiens" might further the view that an Amiens style played a formative role in the development of Honoré's art.[69]

The question of the direction of artistic influences and the location of stylistic sources is complex, and many problems limit its immediate solution. Without a clearer understanding of the development of illumination, the organization of workshops, and separation of styles in Paris and in northern French centers such as Amiens, it is difficult to evaluate the sources of any particular stylistic group. The work by Robert Branner demonstrates the complex and diverse situation of Parisian illumination between 1225 and 1275 and points to the need for similar analysis and separation of styles for late-thirteenth-century Paris, as well as other areas of France and England.[70] Branner's study makes it clear that, as in Amiens, it is impossible to speak of a Parisian style in general; rather, specific aspects of illumination produced in Paris must be considered. Another

67. Millard Meiss, "The Exhibition of French Manuscripts of the XIII–XVI Centuries at the Bibliothèque Nationale," *Art Bulletin* 38 (1965), 189. For the influence of northern French illumination on Parisian painting in the late twelfth and first half of the thirteenth century see Branner, *Manuscript Painting in Paris*, pp. 26–27, 30–32.
68. The Walters Art Gallery, *Illuminated Books*, p. 24; Erwin Panofsky, *Early Netherlandish Painting* (Cambridge, Mass., 1953), p. 15, n.3. Turner, "The Development of Maître Honoré," p. 57, points out that one of the M729 artists was "particularly close to Honoré," but he believes that these similarities represent a "derivation" of Honoré's style in M729.
69. Baron, "Enlumineurs, peintres et sculpteurs Parisien," pp. 43, 50. The significance of these place names is open to many interpretations. See Ayres, "The Miniatures of the Santa Barbara Bible," p. 7, n.11.
70. Branner, *Manuscript Painting in Paris*. For styles in the third quarter of the thirteenth century see pp. 97–141.

complication arises from the absence of firm dates for most of these manuscripts. Without knowing whether one manuscript is earlier or later than another, the direction of stylistic influence cannot be determined with certainty.

Assessing M729's relationship to Parisian manuscripts such as the British Library Evangeliary and other manuscripts attributed to Honoré's oeuvre illustrates some of these difficulties. First, the painting attributed to Master Honoré is one of several late-thirteenth-century Parisian styles that lacks clear definition. Despite many discussions of Honoré's work based on several well-known manuscripts, these comments have not adequately accounted for the stylistic diversity among the various manuscripts attributed to Honoré and even within the individual manuscripts themselves.[71] The manuscripts thought to be examples of Honoré's work represent outstanding achievements of Parisian illumination in the late thirteenth century, but without an explanation of the stylistic relationships between them, based on thorough codicological and stylistic analysis, it is premature to point to sources and influences for the origin and development of this illumination.[72]

The problem of dating also arises, as in the case of the Evangeliary, Add. 17341. Some descriptions of the Evangeliary place its illumination around 1275.[73] In other studies, the manuscript has been dated later, around 1285 to 1290.[74] If the date is closer to 1275, this Evangeliary and other manuscripts of similar date such as the Saint-Germain Martyrol-

---

71. F. de Mély, "Le Miniaturiste Parisien Honoré," *La Revue de l'Art Ancien et Moderne* 28, pt. 1 (1910), 345–358. De Mély pointed out differences in style within the manuscript most securely attributed to Honoré, the Decretals of Gratian in Tours, MS 588, and also stylistic variations among other works attributed to Honoré. Victor Leroquais, *Les Bréviaires manuscrits des bibliothèques publiques de France,* 2 (Paris, 1934), 465–468, also remarked on stylistic dissimilarities between the Gratian, Tours MS 588, and the Breviary of Philippe le Bel, Bibliothèque Nationale lat. 1023. See also Ellen Kosmer, "Master Honoré: A Reconsideration of the Documents," *Gesta* 14 (1975), 66.

72. Ayres, "The Miniatures of the Santa Barbara Bible," p. 8; Kosmer, "Master Honoré," p. 66. Kosmer re-evaluates the Honoré question in light of the documentary evidence and concludes that these manuscripts must be submitted to "the minute stylistic inquiry which alone can establish a master's oeuvre."

73. The National Gallery of Canada, *Art and the Courts,* 1:76.

74. Schmidt, "Materialien zur französischen Buchmalerei," p. 163, n.23, has suggested that a date of 1275 may be about 10 years too early. This redating would place Add. 17341 around 1285. Branner, *Manuscript Painting in Paris,* p. 137, dates this Evangeliary around 1290.

ogy could provide a stylistic source or antecedent for M729.[75] If, on the other hand, Add. 17341 is dated around 1290, it probably would be later than M729, and the direction of stylistic influence could be reversed. Since the resolution of problems concerning the larger development of illumination in both Amiens and Paris lies beyond the scope of this study, an informed decision about M729's artistic sources or influence must await the results of future studies.

Although many aspects of illumination in Paris and northern France in the late thirteenth century need further clarification, stylistic analysis and comparisons based on the Psalter and Hours of Yolande of Soissons add several important elements to an understanding of French illumination in this period. First, the group of manuscripts of which the Psalter and Hours of Yolande of Soissons is an outstanding representative shows one characteristic style of illumination from Amiens in the later thirteenth century. M729 presents the best, and probably earliest, artistic example of this illumination, but the other related manuscripts offer significant evidence of a continuing stylistic tradition whose essential features were repeated with variations in quality and elaboration of motifs for many years. In addition, the types of manuscripts that this *atelier* produced indicate that this workshop specialized in the decoration of liturgical or devotional books for religious houses or private patrons.[76] Second, a comparison of this Amiens style with other illustrated manuscripts localized at Amiens at this period demonstrates the importance of this city in the production of decorated manuscripts in the second half of the thirteenth century. The existence of a variety of styles, combined with the literary interests of some of this city's citizens, indicates that Amiens was a flourishing center for manuscript illumination when vernacular romance began to be illustrated and when books for the laity, such as Books of Hours,

75. The Martyrology of St.-Germain-des-Prés can be dated between 1255 and 1278 by entries in the manuscript. Branner, *Manuscript Painting in Paris,* favors a date in the 1270s. On page 136, he dates the Martyrology "about 1270," while on page 239, he gives a date of 1278–1279 with a question mark.
76. The *Livre de Sidrach* is the only manuscript in this group that is not a liturgical or private devotional text. The didactic character of this work, however, relates this text to instructional and devotional writings popular with the lay audience. This view of this workshop's production may be partially dependent on the accidents of manuscript survival. Also, the six manuscripts selected for comparison with M729 may not represent a complete list of this workshop's oeuvre. However, even the addition of different types of illustrated texts to the group would not alter the fact that Psalters, Missals, and Books of Hours constituted a major part of this workshop's production.

began to appear. However, the liturgical character of manuscripts in the M729 group helps to balance the impression, fostered by Loomis and McGrath, of the secular nature of Amiens manuscript production. Finally, the resemblances between the Psalter and Hours of Yolande of Soissons and styles of Parisian illumination found in the Saint-Germain Martyrology and the British Library Evangeliary suggest a connection between the manuscript decoration in Paris and in Amiens. Although the direction of stylistic influence remains an open question, the relationship between M729 and certain Parisian manuscripts confirms a close community and interaction of artistic styles between the Picard city of Amiens and the center of the French court at Paris.

III

ICONOGRAPHIC PROBLEMS

THE MINIATURE CYCLES

The thirty-nine full-page miniatures and sixty-four historiated initials in the Psalter and Hours of Yolande of Soissons present an extensive iconographical program. Most of the illumination can be grouped into five cycles: the prefatory miniatures, the Psalter miniatures, and those accompanying the Hours of the Virgin, the Hours of the Holy Spirit, and the Hours of the Cross (Table 3). Except for the individual full-page prefatory miniatures, the usual arrangement places a full-page miniature on the verso side of a folio facing an historiated initial on the recto side of the next folio. This distribution gives the Psalter and Hours cycles both a miniature and an initial at each division. Examination of the iconographical cycles in M729 not only will show how the illustration relates to traditions for illuminating Psalters and Books of Hours but also will suggest subjects for missing pictures and an alternative sequence for some of the extant miniatures.

Decoration in medieval Psalters usually occupied three positions: the calendar, a separate series of miniatures preceding the Psalms, and the illustration within the Psalter text.[1] Labors of the month and signs of the zodiac provided the usual subjects for calendar decoration. The prefatory miniatures, however, were more varied. At their high point in the twelfth and thirteenth centuries, these cycles, whose length and arrangement differed widely, included scenes from the Old and New Testaments and representations of saints.[2] Placement of illustrations within the Psalter text itself followed five systems based on liturgical divisions of the Psalms. The three-part division (Psalms 1, 50, 101) was favored in England, while an eight-part division (Psalms 1, 26, 38, 52, 68, 80, 97, 109) was predomi-

---

1. Victor Leroquais, *Les Psautiers manuscrits latins des bibliothèques publiques de France*, 1 (Macon, 1940–41), p. lxxxvi.
2. Leroquais, *Les Psautiers*, 1:lxxxvii–lxxxviii; Isa Ragusa, "A Gothic Psalter in Princeton: Garrett MS. 35," Ph.D. Dissertation (New York University, 1966), pp. 7–35, 39–40.

Table 3: ILLUSTRATIONS IN M729

PREFATORY CYCLE

Miniatures
Yolande of Soissons with Her Family, fol. 1v
St. Francis Preaching to the Birds, fol. 2r
The Invention of the Body of St. Firmin, fol. 3r
Crucifixion, fol. 4v
Christ in Majesty, fol. 5r
Noli me tangere, fol. 6v
Harrowing of Hell, fol. 7r

CALENDAR
Labors of the Months and Signs of the Zodiac, fols. 8r–13v

MINIATURE
The Holy Face, fol. 15r

PSALTER

	Miniatures	*Initials*
Ps. 1	missing	David playing the organ, David and Goliath, fol. 16r
Ps. 26	Temptation on the Temple, fol. 39v	David looking to God, fol. 40r
Ps. 38	Temptation on the Mountain, fol. 55v	David pointing to his mouth, fol. 56r
Ps. 52	Raising of Lazarus, fol. 70v	The fool, fol. 71r
Ps. 68	Miracle of the Loaves, fol. 85v	David in the water, fol. 86r
Ps. 80	Healing the Blind Man at the Pool of Siloam, fol. 104v	David playing bells, fol. 105r
Ps. 97	Woman Taken in Adultery, fol. 122v	Priests singing, fol. 123r
Ps. 109	Baptism of Christ, fol. 141v	God and Christ, fol. 142r
Litany		Priests singing, fol. 196r

HOURS OF THE VIRGIN

Matins	Yolande of Soissons Kneeling, fol. 232v	Annunciation, fol. 233r
Lauds	Nativity, fol. 246v	Circumcision, fol. 247r Suffrages, fols. 253v–263r. For subjects see Appendix D
Prime	Annunciation to the Shepherds, fol. 267v	Magi before Herod, fol. 268r
Tierce	Adoration of the Magi, fol. 275v	Dream of the Magi, fol. 276r
Sext	Presentation in the Temple, fol. 282v	Flight into Egypt, fol. 283r
Nones	Cornfield Legend, fol. 289v	Flight into Egypt with falling idols, fol. 290r

Miniatures		*Initials*
Vespers	Massacre of the Innocents, fol. 296v	Christ with the doctors in the temple, fol. 297r
Compline	Death of the Virgin, fol. 305v	Coronation of the Virgin, fol. 306r

HOURS OF THE HOLY SPIRIT

Matins	missing	missing
Lauds	no miniature	Apostles kneeling, fol. 228v
Prime	Separation of Land and Water, fol. 264v	Apostles kneeling, fol. 265r
Tierce	Creation of Plants, fol. 272v	Pentecost, fol. 273r
Sext	Creation of the Sun and Moon, fol. 279v	Saints Peter and John preaching, fol. 280r
Nones	Creation of the Birds and Beasts, fol. 286v	Peter healing a lame man, fol. 287r
	St. Christopher, fol. 288v	
Vespers	Creation of Eve, fol. 293v	Peter and John baptizing, fol. 294r
Compline	God Enthroned Surrounded by the Living Creatures, fol. 302v	Peter raising Tabitha, fol. 303r

HOURS OF THE CROSS

Matins	Entry into Jerusalem, fol. 310v	Christ washing the disciples' feet, fol. 311r
Lauds	no miniature	St. John, fol. 315r
Prime	Last Supper, fol. 319v	Christ in Gethsemane, fol. 320r
Tierce	Kiss of Judas, fol. 323v	Christ mocked, fol. 324r
Sext	no miniature	Christ bearing the cross, fol. 328r
Nones	Crucifixion, fol. 332v	Temple shattered, fol. 333r
Vespers	Crucifixion, fol. 337v	Deposition, fol. 338r
Compline	Entombment, fol. 341v	Three Marys at the tomb, fol. 342r

SEVEN PENITENTIAL PSALMS

	Tree of Life, fol. 345v	David in penitence, fol. 346r

OFFICE OF THE DEAD

	The Unicorn Parable, fol. 354v	Funeral rites, fol. 355r
Commendations		Dives and Lazarus, fol. 384r

PSALTER OF ST. JEROME

	St. Jerome in the Desert, fol. 388v	St. Jerome writing, fol. 389r

nant in France, especially after the correction of the Bible at the University of Paris completed around 1230.[3] Historiated initials usually marked these divisions, but full-page miniatures appeared in some manuscripts.[4] The subjects varied from scenes of Christ's life to a type of word illustration.[5] M729 contains the three basic types of Psalter illustration. The calendar has illumination of the signs of the zodiac and the labors of the months. Seven full-page miniatures precede the calendar, and both a miniature and an historiated initial separate each of the eight-part ferial divisions of the Psalter text.

The prefatory cycle divides into two units (see Table 3). The opening group of three miniatures depicting the owner of the manuscript with saints that may have had special importance for her includes Yolande of Soissons with her husband and two sons (fol. 1v, fig. 1a), St. Francis preaching to the birds (fol. 2r, fig. 1b), and the discovery of the body of St. Firmin (fol. 3r, fig. 2). The remaining four miniatures, representing the Crucifixion (fol. 4v, fig. 3), Christ in Majesty (fol. 5r), Noli me tangere (fol. 6v, fig. 4), and the Harrowing of Hell (fol. 7r), form an abbreviated group that depicts Christ's passion and resurrection. The identification of the miniatures in the first section and the arrangement of the miniatures in the entire prefatory cycle present problems.

Psalter illustration, especially on the Continent, provides ample precedents and parallels for a prefatory cycle that includes saints and emphasizes Christ's passion and resurrection.[6] What is unusual about the Yolande Psalter and Hours is the appearance in this location of the miniature depicting Yolande and her family, and, in addition, the manner and prominence with which the manuscript's owner is shown. An explanation of the family portrait requires a full discussion of the identification of the saint on the third folio and the physical arrangment of these two miniatures. These problems will therefore receive separate consideration below.[7]

A second difficulty concerns the arrangement of the last four prefa-

---

3. Leroquais, *Les Psautiers*, 1:xc–xciv; Günther Haseloff, *Die Psalterillustration im 13. Jahrhundert: Studien zur Geschichte der Buchmalerei in England, Frankreich und den Niederlanden* (Kiel, 1938), pp. 21–22. In addition to a single illustration beginning the Psalter, the other divisions were a five-part system (Psalms 1, 41, 72, 89, 106) and a ten-part division that combined the three-part and eight-part systems.

4. Ragusa, "A Gothic Psalter," pp. 78–80.

5. Leroquais, *Les Psautiers*, 1:xciv–xcvi; Haseloff, *Die Psalterillustration*, pp. 23–27.

6. Ragusa, "A Gothic Psalter," p. 64.

7. See below, pp. 111–114.

tory miniatures. The present order of these Christological scenes is not the biblical sequence followed in most Psalter illustration: Crucifixion, Harrowing of Hell, Noli me tangere, and Christ in Majesty. Since each of the miniatures is on a separate leaf in the present collation of M729, it would be possible to arrange them, still in two facing pairs, in the usual chronological order. The Crucifixion would remain in its present position (fol. 4v) and the Harrowing of Hell would face it on folio 5. The Noli me tangere would also remain (fol. 6v), and the Christ in Majesty would move to folio 7. This rearrangement provides a more logical sequence, one that accords with precedents from other prefatory Psalter cycles.

The full-page miniatures in the Psalter text depict Christ's ministry (see Table 3). The miniature for Psalm 1 is missing, but the other subjects are Christ's Temptation on the Temple (Psalm 26, fol. 39v), Christ's Temptation on the Mountain (Psalm 38, fol. 55v), the Raising of Lazarus (Psalm 52, fol. 70v), the Multiplication of the Loaves (Psalm 68, fol. 85v), the Healing of the Blind Man at the Pool of Siloam (Psalm 80, fol. 104v), the Woman taken in Adultery (Psalm 97, fol. 112v), and the Baptism of Christ (Psalm 109, fol. 141v). The arrangement of the illustrations does not follow the biblical sequence, which places the baptism of Christ before the temptations, followed by the miracle scenes: the multiplication of the loaves, the woman taken in adultery, the healing of the blind man, and the raising of Lazarus. Since the miniatures' placement probably reflects their original order, other reasons must account for their selection and sequence.[8]

The Psalter miniatures relate to their appropriate Psalm in a type of word illustration; a word or phrase in the text suggests a correspondence with the words or action related in the incident from Christ's ministry. The Temptation on the Temple connects with references to the temple in Psalm 26, as in verse 4, "et visitem templum eius." In the Temptation on the Mountain, the Devil's offer to Christ of the glory of the kingdoms of the world, probably relates to the storing up of riches in Psalm 38, verse 6, "Thesaurizat."[9] The decaying body in the Raising of Lazarus could refer

---

8. The end of the preceding Psalm on the recto of the Temptation on the Mountain (fol. 55) fixes its position before Psalm 38. The regularity of the present gatherings of eight through the Psalter makes it unlikely that the miniatures were in a different order.

9. In other illustrations of the Temptation on the Mountain, the glory of the kingdoms is explicitly depicted in rich objects such as a crown, chalice, and pieces of

to verse 2 of Psalm 52, "Corrupti sunt, et abominabiles facti sunt iniquitatibus." In Psalm 68, the fourth verse, beginning "Multiplicati sunt," suggests the Multiplication of the Loaves. The words of verse 7, Psalm 80, "provabi te apud aquam contradictionis," associate the scene of the blind man washing the mud from his eyes in the pool of Siloam with this Psalm.[10] The incident concerning the adulterous woman corresponds, in its action and meaning, to verse 2 of Psalm 97, "in conspectu Gentium revelavit justitiam suam." For Psalm 109, the actual baptism of Christ relates to the sacramental and priestly aspects implied in verse 4, "Tu es sacerdos in aeternum," while the baptismal waters correspond to the seventh verse, "de torrente in via bibet."

Although the choice and arrangement of these miniatures follows a logical system, no visual sources provide parallels for the composition of this Christological cycle as a whole. Some Psalters, particularly from the Franco-Flemish region, offer precedents for the use of Christological scenes to illustrate the division of the Psalms, either as full-page miniatures or in historiated initials.[11] The choice of subjects in these manuscripts, however, does not correspond with the miniatures in M729, and the arrangement does not seem to relate in the same manner to the Psalm text. Although the individual Christological scenes had their separate visual traditions, many of which were developed in prefatory Psalter illustration, the novel relationship between miniature and text in the Psalter and Hours of Yolande of Soissons presents a carefully conceived program for which the artist had no single source or model. The lack of parallels for this cycle of illustrations also prevents an accurate solution to the problem of the subject of the missing miniature at Psalm 1.

---

gold. See, for example, the miniature in the St. Albans Psalter (p. 35). Otto Pächt, C. R. Dodwell, Francis Wormald, *The St. Albans Psalter* (London, 1960), p. 87, pl. 23b.

10. The miniature of the blind man at the pool of Siloam is an unusual depiction. By the thirteenth century, representations of this incident had become rare, and most earlier illustrations show the man either washing his eyes at a fountain or standing beside a fountain. See Gertrud Schiller, *Iconography of Christian Art*, trans. Janet Seligman, 2 vols. (Greenwich, Conn., 1969), 1:173, fig. 518. The only biblical account, in John 9.1–12, relates that after Jesus had put the mud paste on the man's eyes, he sent him to wash in the pool of Siloam. "So the blind man went off and washed himself, and came away with his sight restored." This account does not specify a fountain and leaves an ambiguous interpretation for the term "washed." The miniature in M729 not only represents the washing but also the man being questioned afterwards by his neighbors and the Pharisees.

11. Ragusa, "A Gothic Psalter," pp. 81–82, calls these manuscripts the Liège Psalter Group.

The historiated initials at the beginning of each Psalm division also follow a system of word illustration, but here, in contrast with the full-page Christological scenes, the artist is following what had become a standard way of decorating French Psalters from the first half of the thirteenth century.[12] The Beatus initial of the first Psalm, always an exception to this system, shows David as a musician and David killing Goliath (fol. 16r, fig. 8). The initial for Psalm 26 shows David looking toward God to illustrate the opening words, "Dominus illuminatio" (fol. 40r, fig. 9). For Psalm 38, David points to his mouth, referring to the first verse, "ut non delinquam in lingua mea" (fol. 56r). A fool with club and wafer of bread illustrates Psalm 52, "Dixit insipiens" (fol. 71r, fig. 12). The picture of David in the water looking up to God (fol. 86r) corresponds to several verses of Psalm 68. The first verse begins "Salvum me fac," and verses 14 and 15 mention the water: ". . . libera me ab iis, qui oderunt me, et de profundis aquarum. Non me demergat tempestas aquae, neque absorbeat me profundum." Psalm 80, "Exultate Deo," names several musical instruments, but not the bells that David is playing in the illustration (fol. 105r). Often shown with the personification of music, bells were commonly used to illustrate this Psalm.[13] Three priests singing from a lectern refer to the first words of Psalm 97, "Cantate Dominum canticum novum" (fol. 123r, fig. 17). The beginning of Psalm 109, "Dixit Dominus Domino meo: Sede a dextris meis," suggests the representation of God with Christ seated on his right (fol. 142r).

The remainder of the decorative program in M729 illustrates its second textual component, the Book of Hours. As in the Psalter, both a miniature and an historiated initial begin each of the sections within the Hours of the Virgin, the Holy Spirit, and the Cross. The composition of these cycles differs from the Psalter, however, in that the subjects are arranged in a sequence that follows the biblical narrative.

The illustration of the Hours of the Virgin depicts major events from the life of the Virgin (see Table 3). The cycle emphasizes the infancy of Christ, but concludes with the Virgin's death and coronation. These subjects correspond, in general, to the standard iconographical scheme for illustrating fourteen- and fifteenth-century Hours of the Virgin, in which the order was: Matins, Annunciation; Lauds, Visitation; Prime, Nativity; Tierce, Annunciation to the Shepherds; Sext, Adoration of the Magi;

12. Leroquais, *Les Psautiers*, 1:xciv–xcvi; Haseloff, *Die Psalterillustration*, pp. 23–27.
13. Haseloff, *Die Psalterillustration*, p. 26, n.1.

Nones, Presentation in the Temple; Vespers, Flight into Egypt or Massacre of the Innocents; Compline, Death of the Virgin or Coronation of the Virgin.[14]

The illustration of the Hours of the Virgin in M729 departs from the later traditional pattern in two ways. First, although the choice of subjects, particularly for the full-page miniatures, is like the standard cycle, their relationship to the individual Hours differs. The omission of the Visitation and its replacement with the Nativity at Lauds causes this shift, so that the Annunciation to the Shepherds illustrates Prime instead of Tierce (Table 3). The Adoration of the Magi and the Presentation in the Temple accordingly move to Tierce and Sext.

The expansion of subjects to fill both the miniatures and the initials creates a second difference. A miniature of the manuscript's owner at prayer begins the cycle, moving the Annunciation to the initial at Matins. Additional episodes from Christ's early childhood continue to supplement the program. The historiated initial with the Circumcision is paired with the Nativity at Lauds. The Magi story expands to include not only the main theme, the Adoration, as a miniature at Tierce, but also, in the previous historiated initial at Prime, the three Magi before Herod and, in the initial facing the Adoration, the warning of the Magi in a dream not to return to Herod. A similar extension of subjects occurs in the Flight into Egypt, with a miniature at Nones and initials at Sext and Nones. The Massacre of the Innocents illustrates Vespers, with the addition of Christ among the Doctors in the Temple for the initial. The cycle concludes by using both the Death of the Virgin and her Coronation to fill out the miniature and initial at Compline.

The fullness of the infancy cycle causes the addition of scenes that are of interest for the development of the iconography connected with Christ's early life. The three separate episodes representing the Flight into Egypt, for example, demonstrate the trend in both literature and art to expand and humanize the biblical narrative with apocryphal and genre incidents.[15] In this sequence, because the simple representation of the Flight into Egypt is placed in an initial that appears in a previous textual section, the two apocryphal stories comprising the miniature and initial at Nones receive prominence.

14. Victor Leroquais, *Les Livres d'heures manuscrits de la Bibliothèque Nationale*, 1 (Paris, 1927), p. xlvi.
15. Emile Mâle, *L'Art religieux de la fin du Moyen Age en France* (Paris, 1931), pp. 27–34, 145–154.

The initial at Nones illustrates a long-known apocryphal legend from the Gospel of Pseudo-Matthew that relates how the idols in an Egyptian temple fell when Mary and the Child entered.[16] The emphasis in this narrative sequence, however, falls on the miniature depicting the Legend of the Cornfield. This apocryphal story relates that as the Holy Family was journeying to Egypt with Herod's soldiers in pursuit, they met a farmer who was sowing his corn. They instructed him to tell the soldiers that he had seen no one because he was working. As he later responded to the soldiers' questioning, the corn grew into a ripe field.[17] The miniature in M729 tells the story clearly. On the left, two soldiers on horseback point to a man who is sowing seeds on the right (fig. 28). Between these figures a ripe field grows. Since this theme received both literary narration and artistic representation for the first time in the thirteenth century, its prominence as a full-page miniature in M729 indicates that the iconography in this manuscript reflects a knowledge of the most current traditions.[18]

Another cycle of miniatures and initials in M729 illustrates the Hours of the Holy Spirit. Unlike the illustrations for the Hours of the Virgin, these scenes do not form a continuous narrative, but rather pair an Old Testament cycle, the Creation, in the miniatures with the New Testament account of Pentecost and the work of the Apostles in the initials. The Creation cycle (see Table 3) begins at Prime since the first part of Matins is missing, and Lauds begins in the middle of the page with an historiated initial. The sequence illustrates the second through the seventh days of Creation: the Separation of Land and Water (fol. 264v), the Creation of the Plants (fol. 272v, fig. 25), the Creation of the Sun and Moon (fol. 279v), the Creation of the Birds and Beasts (fol. 286v), the Creation of Eve (fol. 293v), and God Enthroned Surrounded by the Living Creatures (fol. 302v).[19] The missing miniature at Matins probably depicted the first

16. Montague Rhodes James, *The Apocryphal New Testament* (Oxford, 1926), p. 75.
17. Sometimes the legend is slightly changed so that Joseph, on the flight into Egypt, tossed out a handful of seeds. The seeds immediately grew, hiding Mary and the child. The soldiers thought that Joseph was the farmer and questioned him. See Hans Wentzel, "Die Kornfeldlegende in Parchim, Lübeck, den Niederlanden, England, Frankreich, und Skandinavien," *Festschrift Kurt Bauch* (Berlin, 1957), pp. 177–192.
18. The extant apocryphal literature does not include this legend, and a French poem in a thirteenth-century manuscript, Paris, Bibliothèque Nationale, fr. 1533, provides its first known literary account. See Leopold Schmidt, *Die Volkerzählung: Märchen, Sage, Legende, Schwank* (Berlin, 1963), pp. 261–262. Wentzel, "Die Kornfeldlegende," discusses thirteenth-century representations of this legend.
19. A curious feature of this cycle is the insertion of a miniature depicting St. Chris-

day of Creation. The initial at Matins is also missing, and the first two initials at Lauds and at Prime (fols. 228r, 265r) show kneeling groups of men, probably the Apostles, which may illustrate how the Apostles returned to Jerusalem after the Ascension and joined in continuous prayer. The initial at Tierce is the Pentecost scene (fol. 273r). The other initials show Peter and John preaching and baptizing (fols. 280r, 294r), healing a lame man (fol. 287r, fig. 27), and raising Tabitha (fol. 303r). The missing initial may have depicted the Ascension.

The work of the Holy Spirit is the link that unifies these two independent biblical sequences and defines their relationship to each other and the text. A logical connection exists between the text of the Office dedicated to the Holy Spirit and the historiated initials, since the work of the apostles reflects the inspiration of the third member of the Trinity.[20] In addition, medieval writers from the time of the Fathers often equated the spirit of God moving across the waters in Genesis 1.2 with the Holy Spirit and emphasized the role of the Spirit at the Creation.[21] The choice of a Creation cycle to illustrate this section thus represents the presence of the Spirit from the beginning of time. Together, these two cycles depict two of the most significant manifestations of the Holy Spirit in the Christian view of world history.

The last cycle of illustrations, for the Hours of the Cross, returns to the pattern established in the Hours of the Virgin in that it offers a continuous narrative carried through the miniatures and initials. The scenes depict the Passion, from the Entry into Jerusalem through the Three Marys at the Tomb (see Table 3). This cycle has several interesting features. At Lauds and at Sext, there is no full-page miniature. Since the initial at

---

topher between Nones and Vespers (fol. 288v, Table 3). Since the end of Nones is written on the recto side of the folio, this miniature must occupy its original position. The page facing the miniature (fol. 289r) contains a memoria to St. Christopher in two hands, both of which differ from the main script of the manuscript and are probably later.

20. In other Books of Hours, the Hours of the Holy Spirit is usually illustrated by either a single miniature of Pentecost or a fuller series from the Acts of the Apostles. An example closely related to M729 is a Book of Hours, Pierpont Morgan Library, M60, with scenes from the Acts of the Apostles illustrating each division of the Hours of the Holy Spirit.

21. St. Ambrose, *Hexameron* 1.8.29 and *De Spiritu Sancto* 2.5.32–36. "Not only then did he teach that all creation cannot stand without the Spirit, but also that the Spirit is the Creator of the whole creation." *De Spiritu Sancto* 2.5.33 (trans. Roy Deferrari, The Fathers of the Church, 44:108).

Lauds comes at the middle of a page, and the writing on the recto of folio 327 shows that a miniature was not removed before Sext, no full-page illuminations were either planned or carried out for these positions. One unusual subject is the initial at Lauds (fol. 311r, fig. 37), which shows a face similar to the Holy Face (fol. 15r, fig. 7) but with *S. Iohannes* inscribed on the halo. There are also two full-page miniatures of the Crucifixion: an historical depiction with the two thieves and a crowd of people at Nones (fol. 332v, fig. 35), and a symbolical version with only the crucified Christ, Mary, and John at Vespers (fol. 337v, fig. 36).

Examination of the illustrations in the Psalter and Hours of Yolande of Soissons from the standpoint of their division into cycles helps to clarify their placement and arrangement. With the possible exception of the prefatory miniatures, the iconographical relationships in the sequences of illustrations show that the illuminations are in a logical order. Looking at the grouping of scenes by cycles also helps to reconstruct the subjects of the missing miniatures. Although the unusual principle governing the selection of Christological scenes in the Psalter cycle precludes an accurate identification of the missing miniature for the first Psalm, the miniature and initial at Matins of the Holy Spirit probably represented the first day of Creation and the Ascension.

The composition of the cycles and their relationship to the texts that they illustrate reveal a complex visual program that, particularly in the case of the miniatures accompanying the Psalter and the Hours of the Holy Spirit, amplifies the meaning of the text so that the illustrations themselves become a form of commentary. While the presence of extensive Christological cycles in prefatory Psalter illustration may have helped to provide a stimulus for the transfer of appropriate scenes to individual parts of the Book of Hours, such as the infancy of Christ with the Hours of the Virgin,[22] the illuminators had to draw on many diverse sources to compile this full, yet coherent program of illustration. Since a study of the illuminations that do not form part of larger cycles will also demonstrate a similar intellectual approach in the selection of subjects that visually expand the meaning of the text, the complete iconographical program in the Psalter and Hours of Yolande of Soissons represents an important, and perhaps unique, visual complement for the private devotional book of the later Middle Ages.

22. Ragusa, "A Gothic Psalter," pp. 90, 92.

THE UNICORN PARABLE

The miniature that introduces the Office of the Dead is of interest because of its relation to the development of illustrations for the Book of Hours and for its utilization of contemporary literary and visual sources. In this illumination (fig. 38), a man wearing a hooded cloak stands in the branches of a tree and picks one of its numerous orange fruits. Three animals are grouped around the base of the tree. On the left, a white unicorn sits looking up at the man, and two small animals, one white and one black, gnaw at each side of the trunk. An ominous gaping hell mouth with sharply pointed fangs fills the lower right corner.

This miniature depicts one of the parables from the Legend of Barlaam and Josaphat. The story is a version of the life of Gautama Buddha that was Christianized in the process of its migration from the East to the West, where it had been translated into Latin by the mid-eleventh century.[23] According to the legend, Josaphat was the son of Avenir, a king of India who persecuted Christians. To avert the prophecy that his child would become a Christian, Avenir kept Josaphat locked in a palace, but one journey outside his confinement made Josaphat determined to search for the true meaning of life. At this time, a hermit, Barlaam, was admitted to the palace posing as a merchant. After revealing his identity to Josaphat, he instructed him in the Christian faith by using parables such as the unicorn story to answer Josaphat's questions. Eventually Josaphat converted Avenir, renounced his throne, and joined Barlaam in the desert.

The parable illustrated in the M729 miniature compares people who think only of the joys and pleasures of life rather than the future of their soul to a man who is pursued by a unicorn. In his flight, the man falls into an abyss but grabs onto a tree growing out of a rock. He sees beneath him a dragon spitting fire and four serpents. Two rats, one white and one black, are eating the roots of the tree. As he looks up, however, he sees some honey that drips from the tree. He forgets all the dangers that surround him and abandons himself to the taste of honey.

Barlaam goes on to explain this story. The unicorn is the image of death that constantly follows and menaces humankind. The abyss repre-

---

23. For summaries of the scholarship connecting the Legend of Barlaam and Josaphat with the life of Buddha and its translations see: Sirarpie Der Nersessian, *L 'Illustration du roman de Barlaam et Joasaph* (Paris, 1936), pp. 6–14; Jean Sonet, *Le Roman de Barlaam et Josaphat*, 1: *Recherches sur la tradition manuscrite latine et française* (Namur, 1949), pp. 57–65.

sents the world, always full of evil and danger. The four serpents are the four fragile elements that compose the human body, and the tree is an image of human life that through time, as shown by the rats representing day and night, goes in a path of decline. Beneath the tree, the dragon of hell opens his mouth to receive those who prefer worldly pleasures, the honey, to the concern for the life which is to come.

In M729, the miniature depicts this parable vividly. The unicorn seems to have chased the man up into the tree, which is placed just at the edge of the ground line while the hell mouth fills the chasm on the right. The white and black animals have almost gnawed through the base of the tree, but the man's attention is focused on picking the tree's fruit. The only variations from the parable are the omission of the four serpents and the transformation of the honey into fruit.

The moral of this story, which addresses itself to the ever present immediacy of death, is appropriate to illustrate the Office of the Dead, but it is a rare, if not unique, choice of subject matter to accompany this section of the Book of Hours. Although the Office of the Dead was one part of the Book of Hours that had no immediate visual tradition that could be utilized for illustrative purposes, the scene of priests saying the Office over the body in the choir of a church quickly became a standard representation for this Office.[24] This scene appears in M729 in the historiated initial beginning the text (fig. 39), where two priests swinging censers and reading the Office stand behind the draped bier with candles in front. Since the allegory of death as told in the unicorn parable from the Barlaam and Josaphat legend is completely different from the more realistic and temporal representation connected with aspects of the funeral rites, it is of interest to inquire how the unicorn story was selected as the major illustration for the Office of the Dead in the Psalter and Hours of Yolande of Soissons.

From the time it was translated into Latin, the Barlaam and Josaphat legend became popular in Europe, as the extant manuscripts attest. Some versions exist as single manuscripts, but the story was also included in collections such as Vincent of Beauvais's *Speculum historiale* and Jacobus de Voragine's *Golden Legend*, both of which contain the unicorn parable.[25] In the thirteenth century, individual parables appeared in collections of

24. Millard Meiss, *French Painting in the Time of Jean of Berry: The Boucicaut Master* (London, 1968), p. 31.
25. Sonet, *Le Roman de Barlaam et Josaphat,* pp. 73–89.

exempla prepared for the use of preachers in their sermons.[26] The legend's general themes connected with the human condition and especially the parables with their moral teachings were responsible for much of its popularity, but other causes added to its widespread appeal. In the twelfth and thirteenth centuries, the Crusades heightened the interest in "oriental" literature. Also, since the chief characters of the story were members of a royal family, it drew a large audience from members of the nobility.[27]

Another evidence of the literary success of the Barlaam and Josaphat story was its translation from Latin into vernacular languages. There are, for example, nine different medieval French versions in both prose and verse.[28] Gui de Cambrai composed one of these versions around 1214 probably for Gilles II of Marquaix (a territory on the border of the Cambrésis and Vermandois) and his wife, Marie de Haplaincourt.[29] Although Gui based his poem on a Latin manuscript of the legend, his dedication to Gilles and Marie combined with his elaboration, using the typical language and conventions of the *chansons de geste,* of Josaphat's military conquests that produced his father's conversion bring this story of Indian origin into the world of contemporary French society and literature.

Certain details in Gui de Cambrai's version of the Barlaam and Josaphat story suggest that it helped to provide inspiration for the miniature in M729. As in the illumination, Gui omits the serpents or asps in his account. He does not characterize the animals gnawing at the tree as rats, but rather calls them *besteletes,* or little beasts. Likewise, the animals in the M729 miniature are small, but they do not precisely resemble rats or mice. Gui also replaces the honey with fruit, and the orange-colored fruits are a noticeable feature of the miniature.[30] In addition, although it was com-

26. Sonet, *Le Roman de Barlaam et Josaphat,* pp. 18–19, 102–103; Lilian Randall, "Exempla and their Influence on Gothic Marginal Art," *Art Bulletin* 39 (1957), 100.
27. Sonet, *Le Roman de Barlaam et Josaphat,* p. 6.
28. For a classification of these versions see Sonet, *Le Roman de Barlaam et Josaphat,* pp. 135–136. For revisions concerning the Champenois versions see Rosalie Vermette, "The Champenois Version of the *Barlaam et Josaphat:* A Study in Textual Transmission," Ph.D. Dissertation (University of Iowa, 1975), pp. 8–10.
29. For an edition of Gui de Cambrai's poem see Hermann Zotenberg and Paul Meyer, *Barlaam und Josaphat, französisches Gedicht des dreizehnten Jahrhunderts, von Gui de Cambrai,* Bibliothek des literarischen Vereins in Stuttgart, 75 (Stuttgart, 1864), pp. 70–71. For the date and identity of the patrons see Edward A. Armstrong, *The French Metrical Versions of Barlaam and Josaphat with especial reference to the termination in Gui de Cambrai,* Elliot Monographs, 10 (Princeton, 1922), pp. 26–39, 40–42.
30. Erwin Panofsky noted this correspondence in "The Mouse that Michelangelo

posed about seventy-five years before M729 was produced, the French version of Gui de Cambrai, which was written for a member of the northern French nobility and which transforms the story into a courtly romance, is evidence of the story's popularity in the cultural milieu of which Yolande of Soissons and her family were a part.

The artist of the unicorn miniature in M729, however, goes beyond mere illustration of a group of specific features by uniting them in a skillfully arranged image that dramatizes the parable in one glance (fig. 38). The eye follows a path that the unicorn's gaze and horn direct upward on the left and the open jaws of the hell mouth pull downward to the right. The bright orange fruits reinforce the attention that focuses on the man's central position at the apex of this triangle, but the tension on the central vertical line between the top-heavy branches and the almost gnawed-through trunk leaves the viewer in no doubt that this fine balance is only temporary. It is also clear that the man's actions will be responsible for tipping the balance. This astute and successful rendering of the narrative aspects and moral implications of the parable raises the question of whether a literary account alone was sufficient to inspire the miniature or whether, and to what extent, previous visual representations also shaped the image in M729.

Examination of earlier depictions of this theme reveals few parallels for the M729 miniature. Byzantine artists used the unicorn parable to illustrate the appropriate episode in manuscripts of the Barlaam and Josaphat story and in Psalters for Psalm 143.4: "Man is like to vanity:

Failed to Carve," *Essays in Memory of Karl Lehmann,* Marsyas Supplement, 1 (New York, 1964), p. 244. The following verses are taken from the edition by Zotenberg and Meyer, *Barlaam und Josaphat.* For the small animals:

> Si vit entour son arbrisiel
> .Ij. besteletes ki rungoient
> Et ki l'estoc entor mangoient.
> Il en nota bien la samblanche
> Que l'une ert noire et l'autre blanche.
> (p. 71, ll. 3–7)

For the fruits:

> Garde en son [l'] arbre, s'aperchoit
> Le fruit ù la douchors gisoit,
> K'à la douchour bien pries atoche
> Desci k'a[s] levres de sa boche,
> Esgarde et voit, à la coulor
> S'aperchut bien de la douchor . . .
> (p. 71, ll. 10–15)

his days are as a shadow that passeth away."[31] These compositions differed, however, from the illumination in M729 in that they depicted the unicorn above, with the man in a tree below in a pit, or used a continuous narrative showing the man fleeing in one part, followed by the man in the tree. In the West, manuscripts containing the legend often limited the illustrations to an introductory miniature showing Barlaam instructing Josaphat, but the unicorn parable was chosen as a subject for sculptural representation.[32] The tympanum of the south portal of the Parma Baptistery, dating from the late twelfth century, is one example.[33] Although the composition centers on the man in the tree, the details of the man reaching for a beehive, the dragon breathing fire beneath, and the allegorical figures of the sun and moon that completely fill out the sides differ significantly from the M729 illustration. In addition to the visual distinctions, all of these representations lack the direct symbolical connection with death and instead are either a narrative illustration or a more general allegory about the vanity of life in the face of passing time.

One representation of the unicorn parable from the Barlaam and Josaphat story, however, comes closer to the miniature in M729 in the explicit emphasis on the theme as an allegory of death. It appears on a relief at the head of the sarcophagus of Adelaide of Champagne, countess of Joingy, who died in 1187, but her tomb, which was originally in the abbey of Dilo, dates from the middle of the thirteenth century.[34] The relief (fig. 63) shows a smiling young man in a tree. One arm encircles a tree limb and with this hand, he holds his mantle in front of him. The other

31. Der Nersessian, *L'Illustration du roman de Barlaam et Joasaph,* gives a detailed study of Byzantine depictions of this legend. For the unicorn parable see pp. 63–67.

32. The illustrations in Western manuscripts of the Barlaam and Josaphat legend need further study. Der Nersessian, *L'Illustration du roman de Barlaam et Joasaph,* p. 68, mentions miniatures in Western manuscripts but does not discuss the subjects of the miniatures or the style. The descriptions of manuscripts in Sonet, *Le Roman de Barlaam et Josaphat,* mention whether the manuscript has decoration but do not describe the miniatures. Vermette, "The Champenois Version," describes the miniatures in manuscripts of this version.

33. George Henderson Crichton, *Romanesque Sculpture in Italy* (London, 1954), pp. 66–69, pl. 34.

34. Louise Pillion, "Un Tombeau francais du 13e siècle et l'apologue de Barlaam sur la vie humaine," *La Revue de l'art ancien et moderne* 28, part 2 (1910), 321–334; Willibald Sauerländer, *Gothic Sculpture in France, 1140–1270,* trans. Janet Sandheimer (London, 1972), p. 506, pl. 295. Pillion dates the work by the costume and style of the architecture between 1250 and 1260. Sauerländer relates the style to the last phase of Reims west and dates the tomb around 1260.

arm is damaged, but he probably held a fruit or some honey. At the foot of the tree, two small animals bite the trunk.

Comparison of this scene with the miniature in M729 reveals differences as well as similarities. The most obvious difference is that the sculptor omits the unicorn and the hell mouth. The relief resembles the miniature in its concentration of the parable's narrative into a single image whose focal point is the man in the tree. Both versions give the man a contemporary and courtly appearance. Both tie the moralizing aspect of the story directly to the idea of death, represented by the tomb in one case, and the Office of the Dead in the other. The tomb relief, which is close in date to the Psalter and Hours of Yolande of Soissons and was made in an area of France that is near Picardy, provides a visual precedent both for the type of composition and for the iconographical emphasis on the allegory of death found in the miniature.

The unicorn miniature is an interesting example of the selection of illustrations for early Books of Hours. In the absence of an immediate visual tradition for the illustration of the Office of the Dead, the artist made the obvious choice, later to become traditional, in the historiated initial that shows the performance of the funeral rites. For the full-page miniature, however, he chose the allegorical unicorn parable, drawing on a contemporary story with pervasive appeal in the cultural setting where the manuscript was produced. The story had a literary tradition represented by Gui de Cambrai's poem, which shares specific details with the miniature, and at least one artistic representation, the Champenois sculpture, that is comparable to the miniature in composition and thematic emphasis. If its use in this setting in unusual, the unicorn parable is nevertheless an appropriate choice, and, regardless of the contributions of literary and visual precedents, the artist gave it a vivid and original interpretation.

THE HOLY FACE

A single miniature in M729 that also reflects the impact of contemporary literary and visual traditions is the depiction of the Holy Face (fig. 7). An architectural border characteristic of the other miniatures in the manuscript frames the illustration, but the image within the pictorial space is different from the other scenes. Only the face of Christ, completely surrounded by a gold halo, is depicted. The circular form floats on top of the diapered background, but several compositional devices anchor it in place. At the top and sides, the halo extends just to the edge of the architectural members, so that the columns and arches seem to lock it into the interior space. The curling strands of Christ's hair extend to the bottom corners to form a buttress-like support for the circular form above. The perfectly symmetrical, static composition fixes the viewer's attention directly on Christ's features at the center of the miniature. The face itself, with the modeled brow and cheeks, dark eyebrows, and above all, the staring eyes, presents a powerful, commanding image.

The relationship of this miniature to its accompanying text and the placement of text and illumination within the manuscript are as unusual as the image itself. The text is a short office inspired by the relic of Veronica's veil. As the rubric in M729 indicates, Pope Innocent III instituted this devotion along with an indulgence for its recitation.[35] In M729, the text occupies the verso side of one folio (fol. 14v), while the miniature is on the recto side of another leaf (fol. 15r). Both leaves are blank on the reverse side and separate from any other gatherings in the manuscript. The prayer and miniature thus form a self-contained devotional unit that was planned to appear on facing leaves, but their present position between the calendar and the Psalter, although a logical placement, may not necessarily represent their original position in M729.

The prayer explains that the miniature represents the image of Christ's face impressed upon a cloth owned by the woman known as Veronica. The Veronica legend had many variations in the Middle Ages. It usually formed part of two narratives known in Latin as the *Cura Sanitatis Tiberii* and the *Vindicta Salvatoris*.[36] In brief, the Veronica story relates that the Roman

---

35. The text of this office in M729 is: "(Rubric) Ynnocens li papes de Rome fist cheste orison en remision de tous pecheurs quiconkes dira cheste orison au sacrement il ara .lx. iours de pardon. (Rubric) Psalmus David. Deus misereatur nostri. Signatum est. Fac mecum signum in bono ut videant qui oderunt me quam tu Domine adiuvisti me et consolatus es me. (Rubric) Orato [sic]. Deus qui nobis signatis vultus tui lumine memoriale tuum ad instanciam Veronice ymaginem tuam sudario impressam relinquere voluisti, per passionem et crucem tuam et sanctum sudarium tuum tribue nobis, ut ita nunc in terris per speculum in enygmate venerari adorare honorare ipsam valeamus ut te tunc facie ad faciem venientem super nos iudicem securi videamus Dominum nostrum Jesum Christum. Amen."

36. Ernst von Dobschütz, *Christusbilder: Untersuchungen zur christlichen Legende* (Leipzig, 1899), pp. 205–217; Edgar Hennecke, *New Testament Apocrypha*, 1 (Philadelphia, 1963), p. 484. For the text of the *Cura Sanitatis Tiberii* see Dobschütz, *Christusbilder*, pp. 157**–203**, and for the *Vindicta Salvatoris* see Constantine Tischendorf, *Evangelia Apocrypha* (Leipzig, 1876), pp. 471–486. The Veronica story also was included in some of the Pilate legends such as the *Mors Pilati*. See Tischendorf, *Evangelia Apocrypha*, pp. 456–458. It was also re-

emperor Tiberius, who was ill, hearing of the miraculous cures that Jesus had affected in Jerusalem, sent a man named Volusian to bring Jesus back to Rome. By this time, Pilate had put Christ to death, but Volusian met Veronica, who had an image of Jesus that was made when he pressed his face on a cloth. Veronica and Volusian returned to Rome with this picture, and Tiberius regained his health after he was shown the image. The story usually continues with either the death of Pilate in Rome or the destruction of Jerusalem.

The Veronica legend was retold in a number of vernacular languages. There is an Anglo-Saxon version, and several German versions date from the twelfth century.[37] In French the Veronica story was recounted in several forms, as part of the *Venjance Nostre Seigneur*, of which there are numerous variations in both verse and prose,[38] and in Robert de Boron's *Estoire dou Graal.*[39]

---

counted in the *Legenda aurea* in Chapter 51 on Christ's Passion. See Th. Graesse, ed. *Jacobi a Voragine, Legenda Aurea,* 3rd ed. (Leipzig, 1890), pp. 232–235. From around 1300, the Veronica legend was given a new interpretation. As related in Roger d'Argenteuil's Bible in French, the imprint of Christ's face on Veronica's cloth was made when she gave it to Christ to dry his face as he carried the cross to Calvary. See Dobschütz, *Christusbilder,* p. 304*. This Veronica legend became the sixth station in the way of the Cross. The visual iconography also changed to show the face of the suffering Christ with the crown of thorns and blood running down the face. See Schiller, *Iconography of Christian Art,* 2:78.

37. For the Anglo-Saxon version see C. W. Goodwin, *Anglo-Saxon Legends of St. Andrew and St. Veronica* (Cambridge, 1851), pp. 26–46; Wilhelm Grimm, "Die Sage vom Ursprung der Christusbilder," *Abhandlungen der königlichen Akademie der Wissenschaften zu Berlin,* Philos.-hist. Klasse (1842), pp. 124–126; Dobschütz, *Christusbilder,* p. 278*; Arturo Graf, *Roma nella memoria e nella immaginazioni del Medio Evo* (Turin, 1923), p. 324. For the German versions see Josef Palme, *Die deutschen Veronicalegenden des XII. Jahrhunderts: Ihr Verhältnis untereinander und zu den Quellen* (Prague, 1892); Grimm, "Die Sage," pp. 126–128; Dobschütz, *Christusbilder,* pp. 280*–281*, 283*–284*, 286*–287*, Graf, *Roma,* pp. 323–325.

38. Dobschütz, *Christusbilder,* pp. 287*–288*; Graf, *Roma,* pp. 340–373; Loyal A. T. Gryting, *The Oldest Version of the Twelfth-Century Poem "La Venjance Nostre Seigneur,"* University of Michigan Contributions in Modern Philology, No. 19 (Ann Arbor, 1952); Alexandre Micha, "Une Rédaction de la *Vengeance de Notre Seigneur,"* *Mélanges offerts à Rita Lejeune,* 2 (Gembloux, 1969), pp. 1291–1298.

39. William A. Nitze, ed., *Robert de Boron, Le Roman de l'Estoire dou Graal* (Paris, 1927), vv 1003–2358. See Dobschütz, *Christusbilder,* pp. 298*–290*; Graf, *Roma,* pp. 315–317. For Robert de Boron's sources see Pierre Le Gentil, "The Work of Robert de Boron and the Didot *Perceval,"* *Arthurian Literature in the Middle Ages: A Collaborative History,* ed. R. S. Loomis (Oxford, 1959), p. 254.

In addition to the textual elaboration of the Veronica legend, an image of Christ's face at St. Peter's in Rome came to be identified as Veronica's veil, and this association added tangible evidence to the literary narration. Firm identification of this relic begins in the twelfth century.[40] Petrus Mallius, describing the church of St. Peter's around 1160, mentions the sudarium of Christ placed before an oratory dedicated to the Virgin in the chapel established by Pope John VII. He reports that the sudarium was called "Veronica," and that ten lamps burned before it day and night.[41] Pope Celestine III displayed the Veronica to King Philip of France when that ruler was in Rome in 1191.[42]

From the beginning of the thirteenth century, Veronica's sudarium at St. Peter's gained special meaning for the faithful of Western Christendom and became an important object of a pilgrimage to Rome. Early in the thirteenth century, Innocent III highlighted the sudarium in an annual procession between the hospital of the Holy Ghost and St. Peter's on the first Sunday after the octave of the Epiphany. Innocent III was also responsible for the composition of the office concerning Veronica's sudarium that appears in M729.[43] During the pontificate of Innocent IV (1243-54),

40. There are two possible indications of the presence of the Veronica at St. Peter's in the eleventh century. The chronicle of Benedict of Soracte from the early eleventh century mentions: "Johannes papa . . . fecit oratorium sancta Dei Genitricis opere pulcherrimo intra ecclesia beati Petri Apostoli ubi dicitur Veronica." MGH SS 3:700. See also A. De Waal, "Die antiken Reliquiare der Peterskirche," *Römische Quartalschrift für christliche Altertumskunde und für Kirchengeschichte* 7 (1893), 257. Also from the early eleventh century is a document from the Vatican archives recording a "Johannes clericus et mansionarius S. Mariae de Beronica." See De Waal, "Die antiken Reliquiare," p. 257; Dobschütz, *Christusbilder,* p. 278*; A. Pietro Frutaz, "Veronica," *Enciclopedia Cattolica,* 12 (Vatican City, 1954), p. 1299.

41. Petrus Mallius, *Historia basilicae Vaticanae antiquae.* The portions of the text relating to the Veronica are given in Dobschütz, *Christusbilder,* p. 258*, and De Waal, "Die antiken Reliquiare," p. 255. In chapter 25 he speaks of an "oratorium sanctae Dei Genetricis Virginis Mariae quod vocatur Veronica, ubi sine dubio est sudarium Christi," and in chapter 37 he mentions the lamps burning "ante Veronicam X die noctuque." For other citations relating to the Veronica earlier in the twelfth century see Dobschütz, *Christusbilder,* p. 279*, No. 10, p. 283*, Nos. 15, 16, and De Waal, "Die antiken Reliquiare," p. 257.

42. De Waal, "Die antiken Reliquiare," p. 257; Paul Perdrizet, "De la Véronique et de sainte Veronique," *Seminarium Kondakovianum* 5 (1932), 3; Frutaz, "Veronica," p. 1301.

43. For the procession see Dobschütz, *Christusbilder,* pp. 220, 291*-292*; Frutaz, "Veronica," pp. 1301-1302. The office was composed in 1216 after the Veronica miraculously reversed itself after the procession to the Holy Ghost Hospital. For the office see Dobschütz, *Christusbilder,* p. 224. On p. 294*, Dobschütz gives the

the popular hymn *Ave facies praeclara* was composed, and the pope granted further indulgences for its recitation.[44] This hymn, as well as the fourteenth-century composition attributed to Pope John XXII (1316-34), *Salve sancta facies,* were translated into vernacular versions and were often included in Books of Hours.[45]

Beginning in the thirteenth century and continuing throughout the later Middle Ages, the Veronica was one of the most important relics that a pilgrim could view during his stay in the Holy City. In 1289, Pope Nicholas IV emphasized the relic of the Holy Face in his indulgences granted to those who visited St. Peter's.[46] The Veronica was an object of devotion during the Jubilee of 1300, and Dante spoke of "la Veronica nostra" in the *Paradiso.*[47] From the time of Innocent III, pilgrims to Rome returned from their journey with medals of the Holy Face, called, in English, vernicles.[48] Medals and pictures of the sudarium, "vendentes Veronicas," were sold only at St. Peter's, and the artists of these objects were the "pictores veronicarum."[49]

Despite the popularity of the Veronica in the later Middle Ages and the number of pilgrim's souvenirs, it is difficult now to determine what the actual image of Christ's face on this cloth in St. Peter's looked like at this period. According to some sources, the Veronica was destroyed during the sack of Rome in 1527, but a sudarium has continued to be displayed at various times at St. Peter's up to the twentieth century.[50] Since descrip-

text as recorded in Matthew Paris, *Chronica Majora* (Cambridge, Corpus Christi College, MS 16) in the entry for the year 1216. See also Karl Pearson, *Die Fronica: Ein Beitrag zur Geschichte des Christusbildes im Mittelalter* (Strassburg, 1887), pp. 51-53, 69. Pope Innocent III also granted an indulgence of ten days for the recitation of the office. For the text in M729, which is similar to the Matthew Paris version, see above, n. 35.

44. Dobschütz, *Christusbilder,* p. 224; text, pp. 298*-299*; Pearson, *Die Fronica,* pp. 27-30, 69. The indulgence was for forty days.

45. Dobschütz, *Christusbilder,* pp. 224; text, pp. 306*-309*; Pearson, *Die Fronica,* pp. 22-26, 31-36, 70.

46. Frutaz, "Veronica," p. 1302.

47. Frutaz, "Veronica," p. 1302. The passage from Dante is in the *Paradiso* 31.103-108. See Dobschütz, *Christusbilder,* p. 305*; Pearson, *Die Fronica,* p. 42; Perdrizet, "De la Véronique," p. 4.

48. De Waal, "Die antiken Reliquiare," pp. 257-258; Perdrizet, "De la Véronique," p. 5.

49. De Waal, "Die antiken Reliquiare," p. 258; Frutaz, "Veronica," p. 1302.

50. Perdrizet, "De la Véronique," p. 3, and André Grabar, *La Sainte Face de Laon: Le Mandylion dans l'art orthodoxe* (Prague, 1931), p. 14, follow the view that the Veronica was destroyed in 1527. Frutaz, "Veronica," pp. 1302-1303, shows that the Veronica probably survived the sack of Rome in 1527.

tions of this relic from the nineteenth and twentieth centuries indicate that the face was almost invisible, only medieval descriptions and depictions can aid in reconstructing its original appearance.[51]

The earliest records of the Veronica's visual form come from the thirteenth century. Around 1210–15, Gervase of Tilbury gives the earliest evidence concerning the physical features of the relic at St. Peter's. His description in the *Otia imperialia* relates that the Veronica was a true picture of Christ displaying his likeness from the chest upwards.[52] In the middle of the thirteenth century, Matthew Paris produced perhaps the earliest illustration of Veronica's sudarium in his *Chronica Majora*. The portion of the chronicle in MS 16 at Corpus Christi College, Cambridge, records in the year 1216 how the relic miraculously reversed itself after the procession from St. Peter's to the Holy Ghost hospital and how Innocent III composed an office in the Veronica's honor. Matthew Paris then states that he is showing a picture of the Veronica to aid people in their devotion. Beneath the picture, he continues by recording Innocent's office with the prayer that begins as in M729, "Deus qui nobis signatis lumine vultus tui."[53] The illustration (fig. 64) shows Christ's head, includ-

51. The three most recent descriptions of the Veronica are by Barbier de Montault, *Oeuvres complètes* (Poitiers, 1889), pp. 467–470 (recounted in S. Baring-Gould, *The Lives of the Saints*, 2 [Edinburgh, 1914], p. 74) who viewed the relic in 1854; De Waal, "Die antiken Reliquiare," pp. 259–261; Josef Wilpert, *Römische Mosaïken und Malereien*, 2 (Freiburg, 1917), pp. 1123–1124. Both Barbier de Montault and De Waal described the relic as being in a silver frame and covered by glass. The relic itself was covered by a gold sheet, cut out only to reveal the face. Some of the dark hair and beard could be seen, but the face itself was just yellowish-brown with no distinguishable features. Wilpert reported that the sudarium itself had no image, but that a bust of Christ shown to the shoulders was pasted on it in the twelfth century. See also André Grabar, "La Tradition des masques du Christ en orient chrétien," *Archives alsaciennes d'histoire de l'art* 2 (1923), 17.

52. Gervase of Tilbury, *Otia imperialia* 3.25. For the text concerning the Veronica see Dobschütz, *Christusbilder*, pp. 292*–293*. His description of the Veronica reads: "Est ergo Veronica pictura Domini vera secundum carnem repraesentans effigiem a pectore superius in basilica S. Petri. . . ." On Gervase of Tilbury and the *Otia imperialia* see H. G. Richardson, "Gervase of Tilbury," *History* 46 (1961), 102–114.

53. Matthew Paris, *Chronica Majora,* Cambridge, Corpus Christi College, MS 16, fol. 49v. For the text concerning the Veronica see Dobschütz, *Christusbilder,* pp. 294*, 297*. About the picture, Matthew Paris says: "Multi igitur eandem orationem cum pertinenciis memorie commendarunt et, ut eos maior accenderet devotio, picturis effigiarunt hoc modo." There are three other depictions of Christ's face by Matthew Paris or a close follower. On a leaf at the end of the *Chronica* text in Cambridge, Corpus Christi College, MS 26, is a drawing of the

ing his neck and upper shoulders, against a dark background with the symbols for Alpha and Omega in the upper corners. A cruciform halo is placed behind the head. Christ looks straight ahead, with oval-shaped eyes beneath dark eyebrows. The nose is long, and the mouth has a slight downward turn. The lower cheeks and neck are slightly shaded. Christ's hair parts in the middle and falls in waves onto his shoulder. His beard is short and curly and parts slightly at the center.

Two later representations show the Veronica as a pilgrim's souvenir. A fifteenth-century sculpture of the head of a person wearing a pilgrim's hat depicts a vernicle attached to the front of the cap.[54] The face is similar to the Matthew Paris illustration. The hair parts in the middle from a short forelock and curls onto the shoulders. The beard is short and separates in the middle. The eyes glance slightly to the side, but the nose is straight and the mouth turns downward slightly. No neck is shown; rather, the head seems to rest directly on the shoulders. A fifteenth-century pilgrim's medal shows a face with similar features and hair style,[55] but it differs in several respects from the Matthew Paris picture and the depiction on the pilgrim's hat. Two new details are a crown of thorns on Christ's forehead and an inscription of the opening words of the hymn, *Salve sancta facies*, around the halo.[56] The head also lacks a neck or shoulders.

A late-fifteenth-century print in a copy of the *Mirabilia Romae* shows another view of the Holy Face.[57] This illustration depicts three clerics displaying the relic from a balcony to a kneeling crowd below. The sudarium

---

head of Christ dying (head bent, eyes closed) and another showing Christ full face. The frontal face is almost identical to the illustration of the Veronica text except that the cross-nimbed halo and Christ's collar are jeweled. The fourth depiction is probably by a close follower of Matthew Paris. It is on a leaf inserted in a late-twelfth-century Psalter, British Library, Royal MS 2A. XXII. An office for the Holy Face is written just beneath it. It is also similar to the Veronica in Corpus Christi College MS 16. For these three drawings see Montague Rhodes James, "The Drawings of Matthew Paris," *The Walpole Society* 14 (1925–26), 6–7, 25–26, pls. IV, XXIX.

54. For the pilgrim's medals and pilgrim's caps see Perdrizet, "De la Véronique," pp. 5–6; Frutaz, "Veronica," p. 1302. The early-fifteenth-century head in the museum at Evreux is discussed and reproduced in Perdrizet, "De la Véronique," p. 6, pl. 1, fig. 1.

55. Perdrizet, "De la Véronique," p. 7, pl. 1, fig. 2.

56. The medal must be dated after the composition of this hymn in the first half of the fourteenth century. See page 85. The crown of thorns represents the influence of the later Veronica iconography, since the image of the suffering Christ does not appear before the fourteenth century. See above, n. 36.

57. Frutaz, "Veronica," p. 1302, reproduced on p. 1300.

is surrounded by a frame that is wide, but does not obscure the visage. The face itself is similar to the Matthew Paris picture and the pilgrim's medals. The eyes look forward, the nose is straight, and the mouth turns downward at the corners. The hair and short beard part in the middle, and there is a cruciform halo. This head, like the medal, is shown without neck or shoulders.

Although these four representations of the Holy Face differ in detail, their similarities may be taken as evidence for the appearance of the actual relic from the thirteenth through the fifteenth century. The face was shown frontally with the eyes looking forward. The nose was straight and long, and the mouth slightly downturned. The hair parted in the middle and fell in long, wavy strands to shoulder length. The beard was short and separated into two points at the center. A halo was placed behind the head, but the details of its decoration are unclear.

This composite fails to clarify two crucial points concerning the Veronica's appearance. The first question is whether the neck and upper chest were included in the portrait. Because of the evidence from Gervase of Tilbury and Matthew Paris, this formal detail has been regarded as the distinguishing mark of the relic.[58] Since Gervase had spent much time in Rome and other parts of Italy and, in another section of his *Otia imperialia,* had described in detail the topography of Rome with special attention to the basilica of St. Peter, his assertion that Christ was pictured from the chest upwards *(a pectore superius)* is probably reliable.[59] The sources for the Matthew Paris illustration are less clear. Matthew Paris never saw the Veronica in Rome, and it is possible that a description such as the account given by Gervase of Tilbury helped to inspire the form of his depiction.[60] The two representations showing this relic without a neck are later and may not be entirely accurate, so the thirteenth-century witnesses permit the conclusion that the Veronica was a portrait bust that included the neck and upper shoulders.

The second limitation is the lack of indications about the colors and

---

58. Grabar, "La Tradition des masques," pp. 17–18; Grabar, *La Sainte Face,* p. 14.
59. Richardson, "Gervase of Tilbury, pp. 105–107; Joseph Stevenson, ed., introduction to "Excerpta ex Otiis Imperialibus Gervasii Tileburiensis," *Rerum Britannicarum medii aevi scriptores,* 66 (London, 1875), p. xxiv. The descriptions of Rome and St. Peter's are found in Book 2 of the *Otia imperialia.* The discussion of the Veronica is in Book 3. The third book contains descriptions of various marvels of nature and art.
60. Matthew Paris spent his life in England except for one journey to Norway. Richard Vaughn, *Matthew Paris* (Cambridge, 1958), pp. 1–11.

painterly style of the original relic. The only non-schematic rendering of the Veronica apart from the miniature in the Yolande Psalter and Hours is the Matthew Paris illustration, but Matthew Paris did not see the relic, and the individuality of style in facial definition and surface coloration make his picture an unlikely source of evidence about the appearance of the relic itself.

In the absence of detailed descriptions or precise copies of the Roman Veronica, it is futile to speculate about the possibility that the style of the miniature reflects the style of the original relic. There is another tradition that needs to be considered, however, one that is represented by the painting of the Holy Face in Laon Cathedral. The source of this painting is the legend of Abgar, king of Edessa, as transmitted in Byzantine literature and art.[61]

Like the Veronica legends, the story of King Abgar was recounted with numerous variations. It tells that the ailing king sent a letter to Jesus asking him to come to Edessa. Christ responded that after his death one of his disciples would go there. Next, the king decided to send a painter to record the image of Christ. The artist could not see Jesus's face because of the light radiating from it, but Jesus took the painter's cloth and pressed it to his face, leaving his likeness on the surface. Later, Thaddeus (Jude) went to Edessa and cured Abgar.

This image of Christ continued to play a part in the history of Byzantium. In 544, it was thought to have miraculously aided in the defense of Edessa against the Persians.[62] During the Iconoclastic Controversy, John Damascene and others cited this image as proof not only that Christ could be represented but also that he wanted his portrait to be venerated.[63] In the mid-tenth century during the military campaigns in the East under the emperor Romanus Lecapenus, a Byzantine general spared the town of Edessa in exchange for the portrait of Christ and the letter that Christ sent to Abgar.[64] The picture became known as the mandylion in this period.[65] The image was brought to Constantinople in 944 and deposited in the chapel of the Bucoleon Palace, where it resided with the prestigious relics

61. Dobschütz, *Christusbilder,* pp. 102–140; Steven Runciman, "Some Remarks on the Image of Edessa," *Cambridge Historical Journal* 3 (1931), 240–245. The story is also told in the *Legenda aurea* in Chapter 159 on Saints Simon and Jude. Graesse, *Legenda Aurea,* pp. 706–707.
62. Runciman, "Some Remarks," pp. 240–245.
63. Runciman, "Some Remarks," pp. 246–247.
64. Dobschütz, *Christusbilder,* pp. 149–152; Runciman, "Some Remarks," 248–249.
65. Runciman, "Some Remarks," p. 248, explains the origin of the word mandylion.

of the Passion.[66] In the thirteenth century, the Edessa mandylion was included in the group of relics that the Latin emperor Baldwin II sold to St. Louis. By 1241, this image of the Holy Face was in the Ste. Chapelle of Paris where it remained until its probable destruction during the French Revolution.[67]

Since the Abgar mandylion does not survive, only copies or reproductions of this image can give an idea of its visual form. In two studies, André Grabar has demonstrated that, after the translation of the Edessa portrait to Constantinople in 944, this representation established a particular type of icon that Byzantine painting reproduced in monumental church decoration as well as in miniatures and on panels.[68] One of the best examples of the mandylion image of Christ is an icon, now at the cathedral of Laon, known as the Holy Face of Laon (fig. 65). This painting on a wooden panel, dated in the late twelfth or early thirteenth century, shows the basic elements that distinguish the iconography of the image.[69] First, the background for Christ's head is a fringed cloth decorated with a trellis pattern. The cloth is stretched flat, as if it were nailed to a board like the actual Abgar painting in Constantinople. The second important feature is the depiction of the head alone, without neck or shoulders. The treatment of facial features, hair, and modeling could vary according to

66. A number of descriptions of the relics in the Bucoleon Palace chapel mention the mandylion. For these descriptions see Paul Edouard Didier de Riant, *Exuviae Sacrae Constantinopolitanae*, 2 vols. (Geneva, 1877-78), 2:211, 217, 223, 231; Dobschütz, *Christusbilder*, pp. 225, No. 83; 230, Nos. 89, 90; 232, No. 91. See also Runciman, "Some Remarks," pp. 250-251.

67. Dobschütz, *Christusbilder*, pp. 185-187; Runciman, "Some Remarks," p. 251. Among the relics listed in the Golden Bull in which Baldwin II transferred the rights of possession to Louis IX was a "sanctam toellam tabulae insertam." This item has been identified as the Edessa mandylion. See De Riant, *Exuviae*, 1: clxxxi, 2:135. Some of the compositions concerning these relics found in a proser made for the Ste. Chapelle, now in the Library at Bari, include this relic. See René Jean Hesbert, *Le Prosaire de la Sainte Chapelle*, Monumenta Musicae Sacrae, 1 (Macon, 1952), pp. 66, 68, 70-73. Inventories for the Ste. Chapelle also mention the relic. A. Vidier, "Le Trésor de la Sainte-Chapelle," *Mémoires de la Société de l'histoire de Paris et de l'Ile-de-France* 35 (1908), pp. 190, No. 8; 193, No. 19; 279, No. 19; 293, No. 19; 325, No. 18; 328, No. 18; 332, No. 18. The mandylion has been attributed to other churches, especially San Silvestro in Capite in Rome, but this picture is later in date. See Dobschütz, *Christusbilder*, p. 187; Perdrizet, "De la Véronique," p. 2.

68. Grabar, "La Tradition des masques," pp. 1-15; Grabar, *La Sainte Face*, pp. 16-20, 23-32.

69. Grabar's monograph, *La Sainte Face de Laon*, is a complete study of this icon. His earlier article, "La Tradition des masques," discusses the Laon Holy Face also, but in less detail.

the stylistic trends characteristic of the period and place of production, but the flat cloth and the isolated face remained the essential identifying marks of the mandylion icon.[70]

The Holy Face of Laon was brought to France in the middle of the thirteenth century. In 1249, Jacques Pantaléon of Troyes, a papal chaplain and the future Pope Urban IV (1260–64), sent the icon from Rome to the Cistercian convent of Montreuil-les-Dames near Laon, where his sister Sibylle was the abbess.[71] The inscription on the icon shows that it was of Slavic origin, but how or where Jacques acquired it is uncertain.[72] After its installation in the convent, it became well known in northern France. In 1262, the abbot of the Cistercian monastery of Dunes, in Belgium, had the icon sent to his abbey for the dedication of the church, and a number of miracles occurred during the journey.[73] Later documents and pilgrim's medals further attest to an important cult that developed in connection with the Holy Face.[74]

The history of the two acheiropoietos images of Christ's face suggests reasons for including this devotional section in the Psalter and Hours of Yolande of Soissons. The most important stimulus was the growing popularity of the relic of the sudarium that was associated with the Veronica legend in Rome. The prayers, hymns, and indulgences connected with this relic by the mid-thirteenth century extended the fame and spiritual benefits of the Veronica not only to pilgrims who visited Rome but also to all the faithful throughout western Europe. The letter that accompanied the painting of the Holy Face to the sisters at Montreuil-les-Dames and Matthew Paris's account of the Veronica are witnesses of the desire to see an image of the true likeness of Christ's face and the aid that such a portrait could have for personal devotion and meditation.[75] The Edessa mandylion

---

70. The stretched cloth probably reproduces the manner in which the mandylion was mounted at Constantinople. From the fourteenth century, the cloth was shown suspended and accordingly draped in a pattern of folds. See Grabar, *La Sainte Face,* p. 16. For the form of a mask without neck or shoulders see pp. 33–35.

71. Grabar, *La Sainte Face,* pp. 7–9.

72. Grabar, *La Sainte Face,* pp. 11–13, 20–21. Grabar does not localize the icon specifically.

73. Grabar, *La Sainte Face,* p. 9.

74. Grabar, *La Sainte Face,* pp. 9–11.

75. The letter states: ". . . ex ardenti affectu desideratis videre, et apud vos habere faciem et figuram Nostri Salvatoris . . . quodque ex ejus contemplatione devoti affectus vestri magis accenderentur, et intellectus vestri puriores redderentur." See Grabar, *La Sainte Face,* p. 8. For Matthew Paris, see above, n. 53.

in the Ste. Chapelle and the icon of the Holy Face near Laon probably added to the interest in representations of Christ in northern France.

Two of the surviving representations of the Holy Face, the Matthew Paris illustration and the icon in Laon, are of importance in evaluating the visual sources for the M729 miniature. They may recapture to a degree the medieval appearance of the two acheiropoietos images of Christ—the Matthew Paris picture for the Veronica in St. Peter's and the Laon icon for the mandylion in the Ste. Chapelle. More significantly, either of them could have been a more or less direct visual inspiration for the illumination in the Yolande Psalter and Hours.

The M729 miniature resembles the Matthew Paris picture in several ways (figs. 7, 64). In both, the face is shown in a frontal view. In the Matthew Paris Veronica, the eyes are rounder and the pupils smaller, but the straight, staring look is similar. The hair, separated into light and dark strands and drawn in a wavy pattern, is also similar in the two pictures.

Despite these resemblances, the differences between the Matthew Paris Veronica and the M729 miniature are more outstanding. The proportions of the faces differ; the face in the Matthew Paris illustration is broader and rounder than the elongated, rectangular head in M729. Several details are also dissimilar. The nose is perfectly frontal in M729, while the Matthew Paris nose is shown in a three-quarter view. The hair is tucked behind the ears in the Matthew Paris face, but the hair covers the ears in the M729 illumination. The beard in the Matthew Paris picture is curlier and does not extend up to the nose. The most revealing differences, however, are the sketchy indications of the facial modeling and the presence of the neck and shoulders in the Matthew Paris depiction.

The miniature in the Yolande Psalter and Hours does not look exactly like the icon of the Holy Face either (figs. 7, 65). Several aspects of the icon give it a more natural, less intense appearance. The eyes glance to one side, and the hair and beard are more flowing and smooth. The dark tones of the hair and skin blend together, in contrast to the clear separation of the dark brown hair and lighter brown face in the miniature. Some details are also different. The M729 illumination lacks the illusion of the cloth background as well as the jewels on the halo's cross arms.

There are, however, significant resemblances between these two images of Christ's face. Both heads are long and narrow, and the hair covers the ears in a semi-circular pattern. The modeling techniques share the same smooth, painterly transition between tones, giving a three-dimensional illusion to the heads. The modeling also repeats the same patterns: the

V-shaped furrows on the brow, the straight highlight down the center of the nose, the light accentuation of the cheekbones, and the two light spots on the chin. Another important similarity is the depiction of the head alone, isolated against the halo and background, unattached to a neck or shoulders.

On stylistic grounds alone, the Holy Face of Laon is a more compelling candidate than the Matthew Paris illustration to have been an immediate visual source for the M729 illumination. Historically as well the Laon painting is a much more likely source. It was housed at a convent near Laon, not far from the Amiens area where M729 was produced. In the 1260s it was transported to Belgium and back, and the miracles and cult connected with the Holy Face enhanced its reputation throughout northern France. Since the text that accompanies this miniature in M729 demonstrates that the illustration was intended to represent the Veronica at St. Peter's, the choice of a Slavic icon for a model might seem both unusual and unfitting. However, there are indications that the icon was perceived, if not as a copy of the sudarium in Rome, as an image of Christ's likeness that would inspire the same kind of devotion as the Veronica at St. Peter's. The letter sent with the icon to the nuns at Montreuil-les-Dames points to an analogy between these two representations. In the letter, Jacques of Troyes compares the authenticity of Christ's features in the icon with the authenticity of the image on the Veronica at Rome.[76] The popular imagination did not make such fine distinctions, and the icon of the Holy Face soon was regarded simply as a true image or Veronica.[77]

The miniature of the Holy Face in the Psalter and Hours of Yolande of Soissons contributes to an understanding of the development of iconographic traditions associated with the Veronica. The purpose of the illustration in M729, which, like the Matthew Paris picture and the Laon icon, was to inspire meditation through visual identification with Christ's likeness, is another witness to the enthusiasm for the idea that a portrait of Christ could provide spiritual aid to personal devotion. The miniature also

76. Jacques's letter says: ". . . ut propter reverentiam illius quem repraesentat, recipiatis eam, ut Sanctam Veronicam, seu veram ipsius imaginem et similitudinem. . . ." See Grabar, *La Sainte Face*, pp. 8, 14.
77. A collection of Cistercian statutes from 1467 speaks of some of the abuses of the customs connected with ceremonies in honor of the Holy Face at the Montreuil convent. These statutes refer to the icon of the Holy Face as "sacra Veronica." See Grabar, *La Sainte Face*, p. 9, n.5.

occupies a significant position in the visual iconographic tradition associated with the Holy Face. It is one of the few surviving representations of an acheiropoietos image of Christ's face in Western Europe before 1300. Although by the eleventh century Byzantine art had developed an iconography of the Holy Face based on the Abgar mandylion in Constantinople, in the West the only known depictions of the Holy Face inspired by the relic of Veronica's sudarium were the illustrations that Matthew Paris had made around the mid-thirteenth century. The image in M729 is one other example of the earliest European pictorial tradition associated with this relic before the Veronica legend became attached to the narrative of Christ's passion. It is of interest, however, that Byzantine art probably provided a visual source and stimulus for this illumination. The mask-like form of the face and the plastically articulated modeling come from the iconographic tradition of the Byzantine mandylion, an example of which was to be found close to the Amiens area. The linear articulation of the eyes and nose, and the symmetrically curving pattern of the hair, which is motivated by an interest in design rather than naturalistic representation, demonstrate that the M729 artist was translating the painterly Byzantine style into the northern Gothic artistic style, which was characterized by the use of well-defined outlines and clear, bright colors. The miniature of the Holy Face thus combines a variety of cultural influences to produce an image of great visual and spiritual impact.

THE FRANCISCAN ICONOGRAPHY

The pervasive influence of Franciscan themes and ideas reveals another response to contemporary currents of thought in the iconography of M729's miniatures. Images that have their sources in Franciscan writings not only form the subject of several full-page miniatures but also add a new dimension to the details of more traditional representations. The appearance of this iconography in the Psalter and Hours of Yolande of Soissons demonstrates the impact of the Franciscan message on popular beliefs as expressed through the visual arts in the later thirteenth century.

A full-page miniature of St. Francis, one of the two saints in the prefatory cycle, introduces this Franciscan iconography (fig. 1b). St. Francis, dressed in his grey habit and displaying the stigmata, stands in the center of the miniature facing and pointing to a tree on the right on which six birds perch. A pelican faces St. Francis at the foot of the tree. Three birds sit on the limbs of another tree placed behind the saint on the left. Since the background is gold, only the narrow ground line and the trees indicate the setting.

This scene illustrates the sermon to the birds, which according to most accounts of St. Francis's life took place near Bevagna, in the valley of Spoleto. He told the birds to praise the Lord, "who has given you feathers for clothing, wings for flight and all that ye have need of." Celano's first life of St. Francis specified that the birds were "doves, crows, and some others popularly called daws," but this illustration corresponds more closely to Bonaventura's life of St. Francis, which mentions only a flock of birds of various kinds.[78] The incident appealed to the popular imagination since it expressed the sympathy and devotion with which St. Francis regarded all natural things.

The depiction of this incident from St. Francis's life follows a pattern found in French manuscript illumination in the second half of the thirteenth century. The miniature in the northern French Psalter of Gérard de Damville (New York, Pierpont Morgan Library, M72, fig. 66) is one example of this composition, which also appears as a marginal scene in other northern French manuscripts.[79] St. Francis, in grey habit and with the stigmata, stands on the left facing and pointing to a tree filled with various kinds of birds on the right. Another Franciscan, probably Brother Leo, is seated on the ground between Francis and the tree, while three long-legged birds stand around the base of the tree. This depiction of the Sermon to the Birds is distinct from early representations of this incident in Italian and English art, which differ in composition and details from these French illustrations.[80] Except for the omission of the additional

78. Thomas of Celano, *The First Life of St. Francis* 21.58; Bonaventura, *Major Life of St. Francis* 12.3. From the translations in Marion A. Habig, ed., *St. Francis of Assisi, Writings and Early Biographies: English Omnibus of the Sources for the Life of St. Francis* (Chicago, 1973), pp. 277–278, 722–723.

79. For the Psalter of Gérard de Damville see The Walters Art Gallery, *Illuminated Books of the Middle Ages and Renaissance* (Baltimore, 1949), p. 23; The National Gallery of Canada, *Art and the Courts, France and England from 1259 to 1328*, 1 (Ottawa, 1972), pp. 84–85. As a marginal scene, it appears in the Fieschi Psalter (Baltimore, Walters Art Gallery, W45, fol. 139v), done in northern France around 1250, and in a later-thirteenth-century Book of Hours for the use of Thérouanne (Marseille, Bibliothèque Municipale, MS 111, fol. 139r). See Lilian Randall, "The Fieschi Psalter," *Journal of the Walters Art Gallery* 23 (1960), 36, fig. 8; Joseph Billioud, "Très anciennes heures de Thérouanne à la bibliothèque de Marseille," *Trésors des bibliothèques de France* 17 (n.d.), 173–174, fig. 9.

80. The first extant painting with scenes illustrating the St. Francis legend is an altarpiece in San Francisco at Pescia, signed and dated by Bonaventura Berlinghieri in 1235. St. Francis and two friars stand in front of a small architectural structure

Franciscan, the miniature in M729 conforms in all details—the pointing St. Francis with the stigmata, the tree with a variety of birds, and the long-legged birds beneath the tree—to the visual version current in northern France in the late thirteenth century.

The Franciscan message had a deep influence on late medieval spirituality that surpassed an interest in St. Francis's life and a veneration of the saint himself. Two of the most important ideas that grew out of the Franciscans' origin and defined their spiritual mission were the principles of identification and redemption.[81] In the Franciscan view, a personal identification with all aspects of Christ's life led to a fuller understanding of the redemptive power of Christ's sacrifice. These two central ideas influenced literary and visual spiritual expressions in two ways. First, the principle of identification placed an emphasis on the human aspects of Christ's life, ranging from an interest in physical details to an association with the feelings and emotions that situations in the biblical narrative generated.[82] Second, the personal quality of identification combined with the implication that this approach to meditation would culminate in an increased comprehension of Christ's redemptive purpose encouraged individual devotions that could reach a mystical and ascetic nature.[83] Several

---

on the left, while on the right the birds perch in small trees that dot a craggy mountain. Robert Oertel, *Early Italian Painting to 1400* (New York, 1968), pp. 38–39, pls. 30, 31. Subsequent Italian versions of this scene varied but continued to use a landscape setting, especially with the small mountain. See, for example, a panel by a follower of Guido of Siena dated around 1275 in the Accademia at Siena, No. 313. Raimond van Marle, *The Development of the Italian Schools of Painting,* 1 (The Hague, 1923), p. 373, fig. 204; Edward B. Garrison, *Italian Romanesque Panel Painting: An Illustrated Index* (Florence, 1949), No. 411. English illustrations often included birds of prey in reference to Roger of Wendover's account of this incident in which Rome, associated with Babylon of the Apocalypse, became the location for this sermon, transforming the birds into the birds of prey described in Revelation. F. D. Klingender, "St. Francis and the Birds of the Apocalypse," *Journal of the Warburg and Courtauld Institutes* 16 (1953), 13–20; Edward Armstrong, *St. Francis, Nature Mystic* (Berkeley, 1972), pp. 62–63.

81. David L. Jeffrey, *The Early English Lyric and Franciscan Spirituality* (Lincoln, 1975), pp. 50–72; idem, "Franciscan Spirituality and the Rise of Early English Drama," *Mosaic* 8 (1975), 20–22.

82. The *Meditations on the Life of Christ,* written around the end of the thirteenth or early fourteenth century, is one of the best examples of the concentration on the human details of Christ's life. See Isa Ragusa and Rosalie B. Green, *Meditations on the Life of Christ, An Illustrated Manuscript of the Fourteenth Century* (Princeton, 1961). For the influence of these ideas on the visual arts see Mâle, *L'Art religieux de la fin du Moyen Age,* pp. ii–iii.

83. For a discussion of Franciscan mysticism and especially the contributions of St.

of the illustrations in the Psalter and Hours of Yolande of Soissons offer important evidence for an early visual interpretation of the principles of identification and redemption as expressions of Franciscan piety.

The Crucifixion, as the climax of the purpose of Christ's life, represented, in Franciscan spirituality, the most important event through which the individual, through meditation, could endeavor to comprehend the immensity of God's love and sacrifice for humankind.[84] St. Francis's life was an example of the spiritual fruits of such contemplation, and his reception of the stigmata added visible evidence to inspire the faithful. Religious lyric poetry, often composed in the vernacular, effectively used the principle of identification to achieve an understanding of the Crucifixion's central position in the Christian doctrine of redemption. Through a concentration on the physical aspects of Christ's suffering and, even more important, on the Virgin Mother's sorrow and grief at her son's death, these verses expressed the Crucifixion's redemptive force in terms readily understandable to a lay audience.[85] The Psalter and Hours of Yolande of Soissons emphasized the importance of the Crucifixion in a visual manner by including four different depictions of this event as full-page miniatures throughout the manuscript.

Three of these miniatures follow traditional iconographical patterns for depicting the Crucifixion and are placed in clear relationship to the sequences of illustrations and the text. The first (fol. 4v, fig. 3) begins the series of four miniatures in the prefatory cycle, which depicts Christ's passion and resurrection. In keeping with its function as the introductory miniature, to illustrate the theme in an abbreviated and direct way, the miniature confines itself to a simple, symbolic image of the Crucifixion. Christ hangs on a slender cross in the center of the miniature. The only

---

Bonaventura see John V. Fleming, *An Introduction to the Franciscan Literature of the Middle Ages* (Chicago, 1977), pp. 190–234, and for the spiritual style and purpose of the *Meditations on the Life of Christ* see pp. 245–251.

84. Etienne Gilson, "Saint Bonaventure et l'iconographie de la Passion," *Revue d'histoire franciscaine* (1924), 405–424; Sarah Appleton Weber, *Theology and Poetry in the Middle English Lyric* (Columbus, Ohio, 1969), 89–110.

85. See Jeffrey, *The Early English Lyric*, pp. 118–168, for a summary of the Italian lyrics, and pp. 231–268 for Middle English lyric poetry. For Christ's suffering and Mary's sorrow in the Middle English lyric see also Weber, *Theology and Poetry*, pp. 89–150. An integrated analysis of the possible influence of Franciscan spirituality on French literature remains to be done, but for a summary of some French poems of this character see Edith Brayer, "La Littérature religieuse (Liturgie et Bible)," *La Littérature didactique, allegorique, et satirique*, Grundriss der romanischen Literaturen des Mittelalters, 6, pt. 1 (Heidelberg, 1968), p. 20.

other figures are Mary, who expresses her grief by supporting her bended head in one hand, and John, who gestures as if directing the viewer to behold the crucified Christ silhouetted against the flat diapered background.

The next two Crucifixions form part of a series of miniatures and historiated initials of Christ's passion that illustrate the Hours of the Cross. At Nones (fol. 332v, fig. 35), the artist chooses an historical depiction, based on the biblical narrative, that includes the crucified thieves, the sponge bearer, and probably the centurion gesturing toward Christ.[86] Longinus, the spear bearer who points to his eye, comes from a later tradition relating that when a drop of Christ's blood running down the lance touched Longinus's diseased eyes, they were healed.[87] The group of spectators and even the small plants growing in the foreground add to the realistic and dramatic setting. This narrative quality continues in the historiated initial facing the miniature (fol. 333r), where a building crumbles and falls to illustrate the earthquake that occurred at the time of the Crucifixion.

Another miniature of the Crucifixion follows immediately at Vespers in the Hours of the Cross (fol. 337v, fig. 36). Its simple, symbolical interpretation of the event provides a contrast to the preceding illustration. Like the Crucifixion in the prefatory cycle, it confines the figures to the crucified Christ in the center with Mary standing on the left and John on the right. The only additions are the symbolic sun and moon that appear in small clouds beside the top of the cross and the basilisk on which Christ treads at the foot of the cross. These details had a long association with depictions of the Crucifixion in Christian art.[88]

86. The presence of the thieves and the sponge bearer is related in Matt. 27.37–38, 48; Mark 15.26–27, 36; Luke 23.33, 37–38; John 19.18–19, 29. For the centurion see Matt. 27.54; Mark 15.39; Luke 23.47. Usually the centurion is dressed as a soldier, but sometimes he wears less specifically identifiable garments, as in a twelfth-century panel painting in the Museo Civico, Pisa. See Knut Berg, "Une Iconographie peu connue du Crucifiement," *Cahiers Archéologiques* 9 (1957), 319, fig. 1. In a thirteenth-century Crucifixion in the stained glass at Bourges, an unidentified man, not dressed as a soldier, stands beside the spear bearer and gestures to Christ. See Paul Thoby, *Le Crucifix des origines au Concile de Trente* (Nantes, 1959), pp. 142–143, pl. CIII, No. 226.

87. The story was related in Petrus Comestor's *Historia scholastica* (PL 198:1633–34), and Jacobus de Voragine's *Golden Legend* (Graesse, *Legenda Aurea*, pp. 202–203). For illustrations see Berg, "Une Iconographie peu connue," p. 320.

88. For a summary of the interpretations of the sun and moon see Thoby, *Le Crucifix*, pp. 29–31. The basilisk is from Psalm 90.13: "Thou shalt walk upon the adder and the basilisk." It appears frequently in ninth- and tenth-century ivories of the Crucifixion. See Thoby, *Le Crucifix*, pp. 50–52, pls. XXII (Nos. 49, 50), XXIV (No. 51), XXV (No. 56).

Although these three miniatures present three different versions of the Crucifixion, each one utilizes established visual precedents to give appropriate emphasis to its place in this manuscript. The fourth Crucifixion (fol. 345v, fig. 37), however, differs in several ways from the preceding depictions. First, it is not connected with any cycle of illustrations, but rather is a single illustration for the Seven Penitential Psalms. More important, the textual source for this illustration does not come from the biblical account of the Crucifixion. Instead, this miniature illustrates a meditation on the life of Christ written not more than a quarter century before M729 was produced and for which there were few visual precedents on which the artist could rely.

This fourth version of the Crucifixion shows Christ crucified on a cross from which twelve leafy branches extend, six on each side. The sign, INRI, is at the top of the cross, and a pelican's nest is directly above the sign. Six figures, four of which are identified by inscriptions, stand at the foot of the cross. On the left are Moses and John supporting the fainting Virgin, whose breast is pierced by a sword. The centurion, Caiphas, and Balaam stand on the right.

The textual basis for this Crucifixion is the *Lignum vitae* written by the Franciscan, Saint Bonaventura, probably while he was at the University of Paris between 1238 and 1257.[89] This work invites the reader to visualize ("describe igitur in spiritu mentis") a Tree of Life planted in the celestial Garden of Paradise, its roots watered by the Four Rivers of Paradise. The tree has twelve branches, and each branch has a single fruit. For each branch, there are four lines of verse that recount a stage in the life of Christ, and each fruit has a phrase to summarize each stage. The reader follows the image from left to right and from the bottom of the tree to the top, with the stages divided into three major sections: "De mysterio originis," "De mysterio passionis," and "De mysterio glorificationis." In addition, there are two prayers, one at the bottom beginning "O crux frutex salvificus" and one at the top, a prayer for obtaining the seven gifts of the Holy Spirit. The reader thus uses the mental image of the tree with its verses along with the second part of the text that contains meditations on each verse to understand the meaning of Christ's life and God's plan of salvation.

89. For the text of the *Lignum vitae* see Bonaventura, *Opera omnia* 8 (Quarracchi edition, 1887), pp. 68–86. R. Ligtenberg, "Het *Lignum vitae* van den H. Bonaventura in de Ikonografie der veertiende Eeuw," *Het Gildeboeck* 11 (1928), 17–18, suggests that Bonaventura wrote the *Lignum vitae* while he was in Paris since most of the early illustrations of the text come from northern France.

Bonaventura's text provides the basic image of the tree with twelve branches which occupies the central part of the miniature in M729. Other visual images of the Tree of Life, however, broaden the meaning with additional figures, and an examination of these illustrations aids in a fuller understanding of the illumination in M729. The earliest depictions of Bonaventura's *Lignum vitae* are illustrations that accompany the text itself in manuscripts of the late thirteenth century.[90] They are usually diagrammatic drawings of a tree with verses inscribed either on or between the branches and fruits. A miniature from a Flemish manuscript of around 1300 (Darmstadt, Hessiche Landes- und Hochschulbibliothek, MS 2777) shows a developed visual version.[91] Christ is crucified on a schematic tree with a single round fruit hanging from each of the twelve branches. The verses are written on each branch and fruit. This image adds several elements. The busts of twelve Old Testament prophets holding scrolls occupy the ends of each branch, and four medallions, two at the top and two at the bottom, are placed beside the tree. In the bottom left medallion, the Virgin swoons against John, and a sword sticks out at an angle from the medallion's upper edge. The inscription reads: "Et tuam ipsius animam pertransibit gladius" (Luke 2.35). The other medallion at the bottom contains the centurion and another figure, and the inscription of the centurion's words at the Crucifixion: "Vere filius Dei erat iste" (Matthew 27.54). The top medallions show St. Peter and St. Paul, and, at the top of the tree, a pelican feeding her young with her own blood, symbolizing Christ's sacrifice, is inside another medallion.

In addition to illustrating Bonaventura's text, the expanded Tree of Life became part of a compendium of diagrams or schemata illustrating various theological concepts that were intended to be read and completely understood by themselves without the aid of other texts.[92] One of the

90. Two early illustrations from the late thirteenth century are found in a German manuscript, Vatican lat. 1058, and in a collection of theological treatises from Bury St. Edmunds, British Library, MS Roy. II B 3. See Ligtenberg, "Het *Lignum vitae*," pp. 23–24, fig. 7, and Lucy F. Sandler, "The Psalter of Robert DeLisle," Ph.D. Dissertation (New York University, 1964), pp. 134–138, figs. 60–61.

91. Ligtenberg, "Het *Lignum vitae*," pp. 18–20, fig. 2; Sandler, "The Psalter of Robert DeLisle," pp. 138–139, fig. 62.

92. This group of schemata is called the *Speculum theologie*. See Fritz Saxl, "A Spiritual Encyclopedia of the Late Middle Ages," *Journal of the Warburg and Courtauld Institutes* 5 (1942), 82–134; Sandler, "The Psalter of Robert DeLisle," pp. 115–122, Appendix E. Saxl, p. 110, proposed Franciscus Bonacursus, a Dominican who became archbishop of Tyre, as the compiler of the diagrams.

earliest manuscripts containing these schemata is a northern French, possibly Picard, manuscript dated around 1290 called the *Vergier de Solas* (Bibliothèque Nationale, fr. 9220).[93] Its Tree of Life (fol. 9v, fig. 67) illustrates the basic features found in this diagram. A crucifix becomes part of the tree trunk in the center of the picture, with the pelican's nest above, and twelve inscribed branches and fruits extend from the trunk. Like the Darmstadt miniature, Old Testament figures prophetically confirm the New Testament texts on the branches, and at the base of the tree the Virgin with sword-pierced heart faints against two women while John and the centurion stand on the other side. This schema enlarges the group of figures around the tree by including Symeon beside the Virgin, Moses, St. Francis, and St. Bernard below, and Joel and Ezechiel above. Other schemata of the Tree of Life might differ slightly in the number, selection, and arrangement of figures, but the basic elements remained the same: Old Testament prophets confirming the text on the branches, and the Old and New Testament figures and saints around the base of the tree testifying to both Christ and the tree. The group of the swooning Virgin and John was especially characteristic of French manuscripts.[94]

Bonaventura's *Lignum vitae*, together with illustrations of this text and the schemata of the Tree of Life, clarifies the meaning and purpose of this meditational image in M729. Christ is crucified on a Tree of Life that, even without inscriptions, serves as a visual reminder of Bonaventura's meditations on the purpose of Christ's life. The figures standing beneath the tree both frame and expand the meaning of the central image. On each side, the outer figures provide the prophetic link between Christ's life and the Old Testament. Moses, on the left, testifies to the Tree of Life, "Lignum etiam vitae in medio paradisi" (Genesis 2.9), and on the other side, Balaam testifies to Christ, "Orietur stella ex Jacob et consurget virga de Israel" (Numbers 24.17).[95] The four figures closest to the tree represent

---

Sandler, pp. 118–122, argues persuasively that the Franciscan Johannes Metensis, who gave a sermon in Paris in 1273, compiled the schemata.

93. Bibliothèque Nationale, *Les Manuscrits à peintures en France du 13e au 16e siècle* (Paris, 1955), p. 35; Ligtenberg, "Het *Lignum vitae*," pp. 20–21, fig. 3; Sandler, "The Psalter of Robert DeLisle," pp. 266–267.

94. Sandler, "The Psalter of Robert DeLisle," pp. 141–144.

95. Balaam is not included among the Old Testament prophets in the branches nor among the witnesses in the manuscripts for which I have either seen the schemata or a transcription of the schemata. He is, however, depicted among the Old Testament prototypes in the Tree of Jesse relief on the second pier of the façade at Orvieto Cathedral (first third of the fourteenth century). See Elizabeth A. Rose, "The Meaning of the Reliefs on the Second Pier of the Orvieto Façade," *Art*

New Testament witnesses to Christ as the son of God. On the left, John supports the Virgin in her moment of deepest grief, symbolized by the sword of Symeon's prophecy. On the right, the centurion symbolizes his recognition of Christ, "Vere filius Dei erat iste" (Matthew 27.54). Beside him Caiphas, the high priest who brought charges against Jesus before Pilate, represents his prophecy that Jesus was to die not for the Jewish nation only, but also to gather together the scattered children of God (John 11.49–53). Caiphas parallels the centurion's position as a person of authority who took part in Christ's trial and crucifixion but recognized the spiritual purpose of the event.[96] This miniature states concisely God's plan for human salvation and encourages the viewer, through meditation on this image, to participate spiritually in this event.[97]

The miniature of the Tree of Life in the Psalter and Hours of Yolande of Soissons, however, differs in significant ways from both the illustrations of the *Lignum vitae* and the schemata, and these differences offer some insights into the visual development of ideas inspired by the Franciscan approach to personal meditation and piety. The M729 miniature lacks the diagrammatic and didactic character of the other illustrative versions. There are no verses on the branches, and there are no fruits. Four of the witnesses carry scrolls with their names, but they are without any explanatory texts. In addition, the number of figures is reduced. The Old Testament prophets are missing beside the branches, and the group of figures at the foot of the tree is compressed to include only the mourning Virgin with John, two

---

Bulletin 14 (1932), 266; Michael D. Taylor, "The Prophetic Scenes in the Tree of Jesse at Orvieto," *Art Bulletin* 54 (1972), 405, 412–413. The prophecy brings to mind both Christ and a tree image (virga).

96. On his scroll, his name is spelled "Baipas." For the identification of this prophecy in M729 see Erwin Panofsky, *Early Netherlandish Painting* (Cambridge, Mass., 1953), p. 140. In England, the prophecy of Caiphas was part of the Palm Sunday ritual in some churches. At Salisbury, the prophecy was sung at the third station of the Palm Sunday procession, and at Wells, the person singing this prophecy wore a different colored cope. There is also a Middle English verse dated around the early fourteenth century of possible Franciscan composition that dramatizes Caiphas's message. For the Palm Sunday rituals and the text of the Caiphas poem see Carleton Brown, "Caiphas as a Palm Sunday Prophet," *Anniversary Papers by Colleagues and Pupils of George Lyman Kittredge* (Boston, 1913), pp. 105–117. For an analysis of this poem and its Franciscan origin see Jeffrey, "Franciscan Spirituality," pp. 29–32.

97. The Franciscan emphasis on contrition and penitence, especially as a result of meditation on the identification with the Crucifixion, makes this image an appropriate illustration for the Seven Penitential Psalms. See Jeffrey, *The Early English Lyric*, pp. 55–60.

representatives from the Old Testament, and two witnesses from the New Testament. The miniature is not as self-explanatory as the schemata, but the sacrifice of explicit clarity for a more unified visual composition presupposes a familiarity not only with Bonaventura's text but also with the expanded diagrammatic depictions of this tree. The Psalter and Hours of Yolande of Soissons, dated around 1280 to 1285, however, is earlier than the known schemata of the Tree of Life and some of the textual illustrations.[98] The early, yet visually sophisticated miniature in M729 thus indicates that both Bonaventura's *Lignum vitae* and its theologically extended illustrations and schema were well enough known in northern France in the last quarter of the thirteenth century to produce the simplified, but complete and concise meditational image in the Psalter and Hours of Yolande of Soissons.

Franciscan ideas in the Psalter and Hours of Yolande of Soissons are reflected not only in illustrations of specific texts, such as the *Lignum vitae*, but also in alterations of scenes with longstanding iconographic traditions. The miniature of the Adoration of the Magi from the infancy cycle that illustrates the Hours of the Virgin presents an example of Franciscan influence (fig. 26). In M729, the Virgin is seated on the right with the child on her lap. The three Magi approach from the left. The eldest Magus kneels before the Virgin and child while the other two Magi stand behind him. The addition of one gesture, the kissing of the child's foot by the kneeling Magus, heightens the emotional intensity of the scene. The artist demonstrates his awareness of the meaning and the dramatic potential of this motif by making it the focal point of the composition. The movement of the kneeling Magus's arm, outstretched to grasp the child's foot, draws the viewer's attention to this gesture, and the inwardly curving poses of Christ and the second Magus parenthetically reinforce it. In addition, the artist places the kiss on the central axis of the composition. The crown that points upward beneath the foot and, above, the container of gold and Christ's sign of blessing add visual emphasis to the gesture.

The appearance of this motif in M729 prompts questions about its textual and visual sources. Particularly through the studies of Emile Mâle,

98. None of the early manuscripts with depictions of the Tree of Life, either as an illustration for the text or as part of a group of schemata, are precisely dated. Vatican MS lat. 1058 and British Library MS Roy. II B 3 are late thirteenth century. Darmstadt MS 2777 is ca. 1300, and Bibliothèque Nationale MS fr. 9220 is ca. 1290.

Italian art and writings have been regarded as the origin for the proliferation of human details that began to enrich the narration and depiction of Christ's life in the later Middle Ages.[99] Textually, the *Meditations on the Life of Christ,* written by the Pseudo-Bonaventura (probably the Italian John de Caulibus) in the late thirteenth or early fourteenth century, provided a rich elaboration of the Gospel accounts of the life of Christ.[100] Included in this work was a description of the Adoration in which the wise men, after presenting their gifts, "with reverence and devotion" kissed the Christ Child's feet.[101] Italian art also offered early examples of this motif. The Adoration scene from Nicola Pisano's sculptured pulpit at the Siena Cathedral, done around 1266 and sometimes cited as the first visual depiction of this detail, shows the eldest Magus stepping up to the Virgin's throne and bending to kiss the infant's foot. The artist used the diagonal line and the unstable position of the Magus to emphasize and dramatize the incident.[102]

Problems arise, however, concerning the relationship of these Italian sources to the Adoration miniature in M729. First, since the *Meditations on the Life on Christ* was probably composed later than either the M729 miniature or Nicola Pisano's sculpture, it cannot provide a textual basis for either of these representations. Erwin Panofsky, however, in his *Early Netherlandish Painting,* noted that Bonaventura's *Lignum vitae* mentions kissing the Christ Child's foot.[103] In this text, it is not the Magi who kiss the foot, but rather, following a description of the Nativity, the individual soul itself is encouraged, in contemplation of that divine presence in the stable, to embrace him so that with lips affixed to the child's feet the person becomes united to him with a kiss.[104] Although in the *Lignum vitae*

---

99. Mâle, *L'Art religieux de la fin du Moyen Age,* pp. 3–4.
100. Ragusa and Green, *Meditations on the Life of Christ.* Questions about the authorship and date of the *Meditationes vitae Christi* are still unresolved. Most scholars favor John de Caulibus of San Gimignano as the author, but the date can only be placed between the middle of the thirteenth century and about 1330. See Olivario Oliger, "Le *Meditationes vitae Christi* del Pseudo-Bonaventura," *Studi Francescani* 7 (1921), 169–183; Cainneach ó Maonaigh, *Smaointe Beatha Chríost* (Dublin, 1944), pp. 328–337. Oliger, p. 172, favors a date in the early fourteenth century, while Ragusa and Green, p. xxii, date the work at the end of the thirteenth century.
101. Ragusa and Green, *Meditations on the Life of Christ,* p. 51.
102. Mâle, *L'Art religieux de la fin du Moyen Age,* p. 18; Daryl Davisson, "The Advent of the Magi: A Study of the Transformations in Religious Images in Italian Art 1260–1425," Ph.D. Dissertation (Johns Hopkins University, 1971), p. 35.
103. Erwin Panofsky, *Early Netherlandish Painting,* p. 23, n.2.
104. Bonaventura, *Lignum vitae,* p. 72. The text reads: "Complectere itaque nunc,

the Magi do not specifically use this gesture, the implied parallel between the historical act of adoration by the Magi and the individual's meditative adoration of the child in the stable is clear. This parallel not only provides a foundation for emphasizing the Magi's reverence and worship with a kiss, but it also enriches the personal and meditational meaning of the gesture for the viewer familiar with Bonaventura's text. The confluence around the kiss of the symbols that summarize the triumph of the purpose of Christ's life—the crown, the gift of gold, and the sign of blessing—add further resonances to the meaning of this image that accord with the theme of the *Lignum vitae*.[105] With this interpretation, the foot-kissing motif becomes more than an example of the enrichment of Christ's life with tender, human details. It inspires in the viewer, with a single motif, the same devotional approach to the image found in the more complex depiction of the Tree of Life.

A second problem involves the visual connection between Nicola Pisano's sculptured version of the Adoration of the Magi and the M729 miniature; except for the common use of the foot-kissing motif, they show little resemblance to each other. In the sculpture, the actual adoration takes place in the upper right-hand corner of a horizontally arranged composition that features not only the three Magi but also their retinue in a winding procession. In contrast, the M729 miniature is more simplified and centralized. A miniature in the prefatory cycle of a Psalter from Amiens, dated around 1260, provides a closer similarity.[106] In this Adoration scene, the Virgin, seated on the right, holds the child on her lap while the three Magi are placed on the left. One Magus kneels in the foreground, dramatically thrusting his torso, arms, and face forward to enfold and kiss the child's foot. The artist establishes a vertical axis

---

anima mea, divinum illud praesepe, ut pueri pedibus labia tua figas et oscula gemines."

105. The Magi's three gifts were interpreted from as early as the second century as symbols of the three natures of Christ: gold for Christ as king, incense for Christ as God, and myrrh for Christ as man. See Marianne Elissagaray, *La Légende des Rois Mages* (Paris, 1965), p. 22. An additional interpretation advanced in the *Golden Legend* is that the gifts are symbols of what we owe to Christ. In this case, gold is the symbol of love. This meaning also reinforces the ideal of Bonaventuran meditation on Christ's life. Graesse, *Legenda Aurea*, p. 93.

106. This manuscript is part of the Boisrouvray donation to the Bibliothèque Nationale. See Jean Porcher, *Manuscrits à peintures offerts à la Bibliothèque Nationale par le comte Guy du Boisrouvray* (Paris, 1961), pp. 31–32, pl. IV. See also Chapter II, p. 54.

down the center of the miniature with the outstretched arms of both the Christ Child and another Magus above the kissing of the foot. The miniature parallels the M729 Adoration by including only five figures isolated against a gold ground, and by positioning the foot-kissing motif in the center of the miniature with the canopy effect of the arms emphasizing the incident.

An examination of the sources for this gesture in M729 reveals that they were of French origin. The closest textual source, Bonaventura's *Lignum vitae,* probably composed while he was in Paris around the middle of the thirteenth century, was known in northern France, as depictions of the Tree of Life in M729 and other manuscripts indicate. More important, a visual statement of the motif had been made, perhaps as early as 1260, in a manuscript from Amiens, and the composition of the miniature is close enough in every detail to suggest that it might have provided a model for the M729 Adoration. While Italian depictions of the Adoration that included the foot-kissing motif may represent a simultaneous response to traditions about Christ's life expressed in writings such as those by Bonaventura, it is clear that the M729 artist based his interpretation on sources available in the area of France in which the manuscript was produced.

The presence of this Franciscan-inspired iconography in the Psalter and Hours of Yolande of Soissons offers several insights into the spread of Franciscan ideas and their sources and diffusion in the visual arts. First, these miniatures help to provide evidence for an awareness of Franciscan piety in northern France, in this case, in Amiens. In the example of the Psalter and Hours of Yolande of Soissons, neither the text of this manuscript nor other types of historical documentation prepare for the Franciscan emphasis in the illustrations. St. Francis is not recorded among the saints in the calendar, litany, or suffrages, and there is no evidence that Yolande of Soissons or her husband, Bernard of Moreuil, whose closest family ties were with Benedictine and Cistercian houses, particularly favored Franciscan institutions.[107] The use of this iconography may sug-

107. The counts of Soissons and Yolande's father, Raoul de Soissons, made donations to the cathedral at Soissons, the Benedictine abbeys of Saint-Médard-de-Soissons and Saint-Jean-des-Vignes. They particularly favored the Cistercian abbey of Longpont, where thirteen counts of Soissons were buried. L'abbé Pécheur, *Annales du diocèse de Soissons,* 3 (Soissons, 1875), pp. 396, 464–479, 535–536. Little is known about Bernard V of Moreuil's attachments to religious institutions, but his family had founded the Benedictine abbey of Saint-Vaast at

gest, however, that either this manuscript's patrons or the compiler of the iconographic program had some awareness of the Franciscan message and Franciscan approaches to meditation. In either case, the illustrations in M729 and other northern French manuscripts provide an indication of a popular interest in Franciscan spirituality in this area of France.

In addition, these miniatures help to identify some of the specific textual sources that inspired a visual portrayal of Franciscan piety. Etienne Gilson pointed to meditational writings on the passion attributed to Bonaventura as a basis for the expanding iconography of fourteenth-century depictions of the Crucifixion and passion scenes.[108] In M729 another work by this Franciscan author provides the foundation for at least two of the miniatures. One image illustrates the entire theme and purpose of Bonaventura's *Lignum vitae*, while the kissing of the Christ Child's foot in the Adoration of the Magi may draw inspiration from a portion of this same text. These illustrations thus confirm the importance, suggested by Gilson, of Bonaventura's writings as a textual source for the visual images.

Finally, these miniatures provide an important link between the mid-thirteenth-century texts and their fuller artistic development in the following century. The M729 illustrations demonstrate that the visual response to Franciscan piety of writers such as Bonaventura began to be expressed immediately in the second half of the thirteenth century. Although this visual response had been recognized in Italian art of this period, the miniatures in M729 and the slightly earlier Amiens Psalter document a similar, and probably simultaneous, development of images expressing aspects of Franciscan piety in France. The Franciscan-inspired illustrations in the Psalter and Hours of Yolande of Soissons thus add visual emphasis to the importance of Parisian and northern French centers in the popular development and diffusion of Franciscan spirituality.

Moreuil in the early twelfth century, and the Moreuil family were vassals of the bishops of Amiens and the abbey of Corbie. Robert Fossier, *La Terre et les hommes en Picardie jusqu'à la fin du 13e siècle* (Paris, 1968), pp. 513, 704; Paul André Roger, *Archives historiques et ecclésiastiques de la Picardie et de l'Artois* (Amiens, 1842), p. 163 n.2. A Franciscan house was established in Amiens in 1233. Richard W. Emery, *The Friars in Medieval France: A Catalogue of French Mendicant Convents, 1200–1550* (New York, 1962), p. 113.

108. Gilson, "Saint Bonaventure," pp. 405–421. He mentions especially the *Officium de Passione Domini.*

ST. FIRMIN AND THE LOCALIZATION OF M729

Among the miniatures in the prefatory cycle, the illustration depicting the discovery of a bishop saint's body is of special importance in localizing the Psalter and Hours of Yolande of Soissons. In this miniature (fig. 2), the saint with mitre and halo reclines in a coffin placed horizontally across the foreground. A small tree grows behind the casket on the left, while several small plants sprout in front of it to the right. Three pointed rays of light emanate from a cloud directly above the saint's head. Three bishops approach and bend over the body on the right, and the head of another person is just visible behind part of the right architectural border.

Although the discovery of a saint's relics was a standard feature in hagiographical legends, specific details of this miniature point to Firmin (Firminus) ¹, the first bishop of Amiens, as the saint represented.[109] St. Firmin was born of a noble family in Pamplona, in the third century.[110] Honestus, a disciple of St. Saturninus of Toulouse, converted Firmin while preaching at Pamplona. At the age of twenty-four Firmin became a priest, and about seven years later he was elevated to bishop. Firmin preached in southern France and finally came to Beauvais, where the governor of the province persecuted him. He left Beauvais and came to Amiens, where he converted many people in that town and the neighboring area. The governor of Belgium, Sebastian, arrested and tried him and ordered his beheading. Faustinus, a senator whom Firmin had baptized, recovered the body and buried in in his family sepulcher. St. Firmin II, confessor and third bishop of Amiens, built a church on this spot.

In the seventh century, Bishop Salvius of Amiens wanted to recover St. Firmin's body, but he did not know the exact location of the sepulcher.[111] After three days of prayer, a miraculous light, "quasi radium

109. For questions concerning the identity of the saint in this miniature as St. Honoré see Karen Gould, "Illumination and Sculpture in Thirteenth Century Amiens: The Invention of the Body of St. Firmin in the Psalter and Hours of Yolande of Soissons," *Art Bulletin* 59 (1977), 161–162.

110. For accounts of St. Firmin's life see *Acta Sanctorum*, Sept., 7 (Paris, 1867), pp. 46–52; Jules Corblet, *Hagiographie du diocèse d'Amiens*, 2 (Paris, 1869–75), pp. 34–53; Charles Salmon, *Histoire de Saint Firmin* (Arras, 1861).

111. There are several accounts of St. Firmin's invention and translation. The most complete version from which the quotations are taken is described in *Bibliotheca Hagiographica Latina*, 1 (Brussels, 1898–99), No. 3008. It dates from at least the tenth or early eleventh century since it appears in two manuscripts of this date: Montpellier, Faculté de Médecine, MS 360, fols. 121v–124r, "Catalogus codicum hagiographicorum latinorum bibliothecae scholae medicinae in Uni-

solis," revealed where St. Firmin was buried. As Salvius opened the tomb, a wonderful odor that seemed to mingle the fragrances of many kinds of flowers, "candida lilia et vernantes rosas, aliosque virentes herbarum flores pulchre," emanated from the sepulcher. The fragrant odor spread not only though the entire diocese of Amiens but also to the neighboring cities of Thérouanne, Cambrai, Noyon, and Beauvais, bringing the clergy and the people to see this miracle. As St. Salvius raised St. Firmin's body from his tomb, a heat, "fervidus calor," came over the area and transformed the cold January winter into a springtime climate, and as the saint's body was being translated to Amiens, the trees began to flower and put on fruit, and the people made wreaths from the branches.

Until the early part of the eighteenth century, the celebration on the eve of the feast of St. Firmin's invention at the cathedral at Amiens preserved these traditions.[112] An official from the church of Saint-Firmin-en-Castillon, called *l'homme vert* because he was adorned with greenery, assisted at Vespers and presented a small crown of flowers to the canons and chaplains. After the response, *Cum aperietur,* incense was thrown on burning embers. During the blessing of the incense, the officiants changed into their summer robes. All these activities commemorated the fragrant odor and the miraculous blooming of the plants that occurred during the invention and translation of St. Firmin's relics.

The miniature in M729 parallels the details of this narrative (fig. 2). The bishop saint's body reclines in the open tomb. Three prominent rays of light emanate from a cloud over his head and point to his body. Several plants of varying types and sizes representing the warm atmosphere and the flowering plants described in the legend sprout beside the coffin. A bishop, probably Salvius, bends over the body. The two bishops and a man behind them probably depict the clergy and people from the neighboring cities who gathered to witness the miraculous invention. The only inconsistency is that people from four towns are not definitely represented.

Comparison of the miniature with the only extant representation of

---

versitate Montepessulanensi," *Analecta Bollandiana* 24–25 (1915–16), 266–267; J. DuBois, "Firmin (Saints)," *Dictionnaire d'histoire et de géographie ecclésiastiques* 17 (Paris, 1971), p. 255; and Ghent, Library of the City and the University, MS 244, fols. 66v–69r, "Catalogus codicum hagiographicorum bibliothecae publicae civitatis et academiae Gandavensis," *Analecta Bollandiana* 3 (1884), 170, 175. For editions of this version see Carolus LeCointe, *Annales Ecclesiastici Francorum* 4 (Paris, 1665–83), pp. 182–184; *Acta Sanctorum,* Sept., 7:31. Another version is described in *Bibliotheca Hagiographica Latina,* 1:No. 3009.
112. Corblet, *Hagiographie,* 2:172–173.

this event that precedes the Psalter and Hours of Yolande of Soissons confirms the identity of this saint in M729.[113] The portal dedicated to St. Firmin on the façade of Amiens Cathedral, constructed around 1225, depicts events from St. Firmin's legend.[114] Firmin, wearing bishop's vestments, stands on the trumeau of this portal. The jamb figures represent other local saints.[115] The tympanum depicts in great detail the invention and translation of St. Firmin's body (fig. 68). In the center of the middle register, St. Salvius, surrounded by a group of people, stands beside the saint's body. A ray of light extends from the clouds above. Two architectural structures with people pouring out of them flank the central scene of the invention. These four groups represent the inhabitants of the cities of Thérouanne, Cambrai, Noyon, and Beauvais flocking to the site. The top register shows the translation of St. Firmin's relics. As priests carry the shrine containing the saint's body, the trees leaf out, and people spread garments and branches before the procession.

Comparison of this sculptural representation with the miniature in M729 reveals differences in composition. The major variation lies in the greater amount of space devoted to the subject in the tympanum relief. Since the incident spreads over two horizontal registers, the sculptor was able to portray several parts of the story in a continuous narrative. In the long, narrow format of the middle register, he depicted the main event,

113. One earlier representation of this scene, on a metal shrine from the late twelfth century that contained St. Firmin's relics, was destroyed during the French Revolution. Descriptions of this golden châsse indicate that is was decorated with twelve scenes in enamel, each depicting an event from St. Firmin's life and legend. The tenth enamel showed St. Salvius finding St. Firmin's body. The eleventh depicted the translation of St. Firmin's relics, and in the final scene people from the four cities were coming to witness the event. For descriptions of the shrine see Corblet, *Hagiographie*, 2:166; Louis Reau, *Iconographie de l'art chrétien*, 3, pt. 1 (Paris, 1958), p. 502. The inscriptions that accompanied the enamels are recorded in *Acta Sanctorum*, Sept., 7:33, 37–38. The Duke of Norfolk gave the present shrine, a Mosan work of the thirteenth century, to the cathedral of Amiens in 1850. See J. de Borchgrave d'Altena, "La Châsse de saint Firmin," *Bulletin Monumental* 85 (1926), 153–158.

114. Sauerländer, *Gothic Sculpture*, pp. 464–465; Adolf Katzenellenbogen, "Tympanum and Archivolts on the Portal of St. Honoré at Amiens," *De Artibus Opuscula XL: Essays in Honor of Erwin Panofsky* (New York, 1961), pp. 280–281.

115. The precise identity of these figures is difficult to determine. See Sauerländer, *Gothic Sculpture*, p. 465. Georges Durand, *Description abrégée de la cathedrale d'Amiens* (Amiens, 1914), pp. 70–71, gives some identifications for the jamb figures. Wolfgang Medding, *Die Westportale der Kathedrale von Amiens und ihre Meister* (Augsburg, 1930), p. 35, also proposes identifications for the figures.

the invention, exactly in the center, and filled out the remaining space with the symmetrical placement of the citizens from the four cities. He devoted the register above to the translation when the trees flowered and people gathered branches and flowers. In contrast, because the illuminator in M729 had to compress all these incidents into a single composition with a narrower format, he brought all the details—the invention, the sprouting plants, and the gathering people—into a tightly grouped whole. The way that the artist squeezed in another head behind the column capital of the inner architectural border demonstrates the difficulty of telling the story in one composition and may explain the discrepancy in the number of spectators.

Despite the differences in format, there are similarities in detail between these two representations. In the miniature, the slight inclination of the saint's body, the pointed rays of light, and the position of St. Salvius resemble, in mirror image, the central portion of the tympanum. The illuminator added two rays of light and showed St. Salvius bending from the waist, instead of inclining just his head toward the body, but otherwise the basic composition of the central figures is almost identical, except for the reversed positions. These essential similarities may indicate that the artist of M729 was familiar with the sculpture on the tympanum and may have used a sketch of the middle scene, transferred in reverse, for the basis of his miniature.

In addition to the differences in format, a consideration of this miniature's position in the manuscript also may explain some of the variations in composition between the sculpture and the illumination. In the prefatory cycle, representations of Yolande of Soissons with her family (fol. 1v) and St. Francis preaching to the birds (fol. 2r) precede St. Firmin's invention (fol. 3r), and these three miniatures form a group of the donor with saints. A small, unified cycle of four miniatures depicting Christ's passion and resurrection follows.[116] With this arrangement, the St. Francis illumination faces the miniature of Yolande, her husband, Bernard of Moreuil, and two of their sons (fig. 1). In this family group, the tallest figure, Bernard is on the left. On the right, Yolande looks back at her husband but puts her hands on her children's shoulders. The boys and Yolande face at a three-quarter angle to the right. One noticeable detail is the way the children gesture. One raises his hand, and the other points to the right.

116. See above, p. 68 and Table 3.

Their glances outside the miniature reinforce the direction of these gestures.

The miniature of St. Francis does nothing to counterbalance this obvious directional line (fig. 1b). The saint faces and points to the right, thus turning his back on the family. Furthermore, the composition of St. Francis preaching to the birds is self-contained. The figure of the saint is in the middle, with a tree placed symmetrically on each side. The tree on the right and the birds that face the saint keep his pointing finger from leading the line of vision outside the frame.

The composition of the discovery of St. Firmin's body, however, provides a perfect counterpart for the family portrait (figs. 1a, 2). The three bishops echo in reverse the boys' gestures. The diagonal line that goes from St. Firmin's head in the lower left up to the bishop's mitre in the upper right forms a V-shape with the line from the lower right to upper left in the family miniature. The children's gestures are more understandable if they are pointing to a miraculous discovery, and this unresolved line combines with the rays of light and the bishops' poses to make the saint's head the focal point. The vertical figures of Bernard and the third bishop then enclose the scene on the far left and right. These formal considerations suggest a rearrangement with the St. Firmin miniature facing the family group on folio 2r, and on folio 3r, St. Francis's sermon to the birds as a single illumination.

Since each of the miniatures in the prefatory cycle is on a separate leaf in the present collation of M729, a change in the sequence of these particular illuminations would not disrupt the manuscript's intrinsic structure.[117] The pairing of this family group with an event from a saint's legend, however, establishes an active relationship between donor and saint that represents a departure from more traditional medieval depictions, in which smaller size or kneeling attitude separate the donor from the devotional image.[118] In the later Middle Ages, the emphasis on personal devotion stimulated by Franciscan piety and meditation, which encouraged

117. See Chapter I, pp. 1 n.1, 12.
118. For a concise history of donor portraits and devotional pictures see Eva Lachner, "Dedikationsbild" and "Devotionsbild," *Reallexikon zur deutschen Kunstgeschichte*, 3 (Stuttgart, 1954), pp. 1189–1197, 1367–1373. Some of these conventions continue through the fourteenth century. See, for example, Claire Richter Sherman, *The Portraits of Charles V of France, 1338–1380* (New York, 1969), pp. 45–55. In M729, this type of donor portrait appears before Matins of the Virgin (fol. 232v, fig. 19) where Yolande of Soissons kneels before an altar on which a statue of the Virgin and Child is placed.

a person to be present at events from Christ's life, helped to expand the iconography of the donor portrait to include a more direct participation in the event depicted.[119] This religious attitude makes it possible to see the family participating in the invention of St. Firmin's body, perhaps representing the people who flocked to witness the event, as a visual inspiration for the original owner to take part in the event through devotion and meditation.[120] An analogous relationship is established between the viewer

119. An example of this approach to personal devotion appears in several miniatures in M729, for example, the Tree of Life (fol. 345v, fig. 41). See above, pp. 99–103. For the importance of the insertion of a kneeling donor into religious scenes in Books of Hours see The National Gallery of Canada, *Art and the Courts,* 1:65. Jeffrey M. Hoffeld, "An Image of St. Louis and the Structuring of Devotion," *Bulletin of the Metropolitan Museum of Art* 29 (1971), 261–266, has explained how the careful placement and composition of miniatures in the Hours of Jeanne d'Evreux (New York, The Cloisters Collection, 54.1.2, ca. 1325–28) provided a visual structure for this type of religious contemplation. In the second half of the fourteenth century, several miniatures depicting Charles V show the king participating more actively in various devotional pictures. Eleanor Spencer, "The First Patron of the 'Très Belles Heures de Notre-Dame'," *Scriptorium* 23 (1969), 145–147, has identified the third Magus in the miniature of the Adoration of the Magi in this manuscript (Paris, Bibliothèque Nationale, n.a. lat. 3093, p. 50) as Charles V. Descriptions of the now destroyed *Heures de Savoie* indicate that although a majority of the approximately thirty-five miniatures with portraits of Charles V were conventional depictions of the donor, Charles was shown as a more active participant in some of the scenes, such as the Crucifixion and Entombment. Paul Durrieu, "Notice d'un des plus importants livres de prières du roi Charles V, 'Les Heures de Savoie'," *Bibliothèque de l'Ecole des Chartes* 72 (1911), 500–555, and Sherman, *The Portraits of Charles V,* pp. 48–49, n. 21. Although these examples are somewhat later and do not parallel exactly the double miniature of M729, they demonstrate some innovations in depictions of donors at this period and point to the need for further study of the problem of donor representations in the late Middle Ages, especially in relation to the personalization of private devotion.

120. On an additional level, it is possible that Yolande and her family could be participating in an annual liturgical procession commemorating St. Firmin's invention. Later accounts that describe special use of greenery, incense, and changing of robes to celebrate the eve of the feast of St. Firmin's invention do not mention such a procession (Corblet, *Hagiographie,* 2:172–173), but some fourteenth- and fifteenth-century pictures may allude to similar specific processions or celebrations for other feasts in other churches. The Adoration of the Magi miniature in the *Très Belles Heures de Notre-Dame* (n. 74, above), not only may depict Charles V as the third Magus but also may refer to a mass in the Sainte Chapelle on Epiphany, 1378. Spencer, "The First Patron," pp. 145–146. In Italy, Gentile da Fabriano's Altarpiece of the Three Kings (Florence, Uffizi, 1423), originally in the sacristy of S. Trinita, includes portraits of Palla and Nofri Strozzi in the procession immediately behind the third Magus and provides a visual analogy for the unified celebration of the feasts of the Holy

approaching the Amiens cathedral and the scene of St. Firmin's invention
on the tympanum sculpture. This similar function suggests that the sculptural representation of the city gates from which people exit to witness the
invention could have inspired the architectural structure that occupies the
extreme left side of the family miniature (figs. 1a, 68). Although these
miniatures are early examples of the intimate connection between the
donor and the image, this interpretation is consistent both with the nature
of the private devotional text in which they appear and with the recurrent
Franciscan iconography in several of the miniatures in M729.

Considering the location of the St. Firmin miniature, comparison with
the sculptural representation reveals other reasons for the compositional
differences. On the tympanum, the invention occupies the central point
not only of the symmetrical composition of the second register, but also
of the entire tympanum, and it faces out toward the viewer approaching
the portal. Thus, the sculptor directed the single ray of light more toward
the middle of the scene and grouped the spectators in rows facing frontally.
The illuminator, while retaining the basic position of the key elements in
the narrative, modified his composition to accord with the miniature's
place in the manuscript. He shifted the position of the witnesses to form a
directional line to the left. He also moved and increased the number of
light rays to emphasize the different position of the focal point.

Examination of this single miniature in the Psalter and Hours of
Yolande of Soissons adds to an understanding of the manuscript's origin.
Comparison with written descriptions and pictorial representations con-
firms that this miniature represents the invention of the body of St.
Firmin I. Since St. Firmin's cult was confined primarily to the diocese of
Amiens, the appearance of a full-page miniature of an event from this
saint's legend would point to a close connection with Amiens for this
manuscript.[121] The relationship between the miniature and its visual
precedent on the façade of Amiens Cathedral strengthens this association.
The similarity of St. Salvius guided by the rays of light finding St. Firmin's
sepulcher in both depictions suggests that the illuminator was familiar with
the sculptural scene and thus had either been in Amiens or was working
there. The close observation of this sculptural scene combines with the

---

Trinity and of St. Giovanni Gualberto at S. Trinita. Daryl Davisson, "The
Iconology of the S. Trinita Sacristy, 1418–1435; A Study of the Private and
Public Functions of Religious Art in the Early Quattrocento," *Art Bulletin*
57 (1975), 324–330.
121. Corblet, *Hagiographie*, 2:175–176; DuBois, "Firmin," p. 257.

rendering of architectural elements from Amiens cathedral in some of the M729 borders to reinforce the association with Amiens as a visual source for parts of the illumination.[122] A consideration of the composition of this miniature thus adds important evidence to support a localization of the Psalter and Hours of Yolande of Soissons in Amiens.

While the depiction of the discovery of St. Firmin's body strengthens the connection of M729 with Amiens, the iconographic content of the illuminations as a whole contribute to an understanding of French culture and society in the thirteenth century. The picture of Yolande dressed in a sumptuous cloak, kneeling before an equally courtly figure of the Virgin, provides a glimpse of this prayer book's owner as a member of the Picard nobility, expressing her devotion to the regal, yet human, Queen of Heaven. The miniature of the Unicorn Parable, based on one of the many Oriental themes that the Crusades did much to promote, demonstrates the popularity of these moralizing romances among the French nobility. The Holy Face emphasizes the important role that the veneration of relics through meditation and pilgrimage played in the development of late medieval spirituality. Some of the illustrations reveal the intensity of religious feelings that the Franciscan movement inspired. The picture of St. Francis with the birds is an example of his love for every living creature. Another miniature expresses the meditational value of the humanizing effects of St. Francis's teaching, showing tenderness and warmth toward the Christ Child as the Magus bends to kiss his foot. Depictions of the Crucifixion demonstrate the sorrow and mystical identification with Christ's sufferings as taught by St. Francis and his followers such as St. Bonaventura. The active relationship between donor and saint that once

122. See Chapter II, p. 26. The architectural canopy over this particular miniature also demonstrates some resemblance to the façade of Amiens Cathedral
(figs. 2, 41). The painted architecture features three gabled arches that correspond to the cathedral portals separated by flat buttresses articulated with
arches on the foreground plane. Likewise, the buttresses articulated with blind
arches are a prominent feature of the Amiens façade. The rendering of details,
such as the reduction of the double arches of the façade to a single one, is
simplified in the miniature, but the basic disposition is similar. In the St. Firmin
canopy, on a second plane behind each of the gabled arches are two arched
openings that, because of their gold color, appear to reflect light like the outside of a glazed window. On the cathedral also, the arches of the side portals are
in front of glazed windows, but these windows do not use the double arches.
Although details are altered and simplified in the miniature's canopy, the
painted architectural structure resembles the overall structure of the façade,
with three portals clearly separated by wall buttresses.

may have been intended for the scene of St. Firmin's invention adds to the visual inspiration toward personal meditation. These illustrations make the Psalter and Hours of Yolande of Soissons important not only as a document in the history of manuscript illumination but also as a window into the life and thoughts of French society in the Gothic period.

The Contents of M729

fol. 8r   Calendar

fol. 14v   Prayer with rubric: *Ynnocens li papes de Rome* . . .
             Deus qui nobis signatis vultus . . .

fol. 16r   Psalter

fol. 179v   Canticles:
             Confitebor tibi . . .

fol. 180r   *Ego dixi: In dimidio* . . .

fol. 181v   *Exultavit cor meum* . . .

fol. 182v   *Cantemus Domino gloriose enim* . . .

fol. 184r   *Domine audivi auditionem tuam* . . .

fol. 186r   *Audite celi* . . .

fol. 190r   *Te Deum laudamus* . . .

fol. 191r   *Benedicite omnia opera* . . .

fol. 192v   *Benedictus Dominus Deus* . . .

fol. 193r   *Quicumque vult salvus esse* . . .

fol. 196r   Litany

fol. 200v   Prayer: *Deus cui proprium est misereri semper* . . .

fol. 200v   Prayer: *Omnipotens sempiterne Deus qui facis mirabilia magna* . . .

fol. 201r   Prayer: *Pretende Domine famulis et famulabus tuis* . . .

fol. 201r   Prayer: *Pax Christi que exasperat omnem sensum convertat cor .N. cum vera pace* . . .

fol. 201v   Prayer: *In presentia corporis et sanguinis tui Domine Iesu Christi commendo animam meam* . . .

fol. 202v   Prayer with rubric: *Chi comenche l'enquisisions Saint Augustin* . . .
             Domine Iesu Christi qui in hunc mundum propter nos de sinu patris advenisti . . .

fol. 206v   Prayer: *Concede quesumus omnipotens Deus ut intercessio nos sancte Dei genitricis Marie* . . .

fol. 207r   Prayer with rubric: *Orison bone a dire pour cui convient. R.N. ie vous comant a Dieu* . . .

fol. 207v   Prayer: *En la sainte crois soit devant vous* . . .

fol. 208v   Prayer with rubric: *Chi commenche l'orison Saint Gille* . . .
             Deus summe pacis et celi sancte pater omnipotens eterne Deus precor te . . .

fol. 211v   Prayer: *Deus propitius esto michi peccatori peccatrisi famule tue famuli tui* . . .

fol. 212v   Prayer: *O intemerata et in eternum benedica specialis* . . .

fol. 214r   Gospel lesson from John

fol. 214v   Prayer: *Pater in manus tuas commendo spiritum meum* . . .

fol. 215r   Prayer: *Domine Iesu Christe pastor bone* . . .

fol. 217r   Fifteen Joys of the Virgin
             Douche dame de misericorde, mere de pitié . . .

fol. 220r   Poem to the Virgin: *Dame resplendisans, roïne glorieuse* . . .

fol. 223r   Hours of the Holy Spirit and Hours of the Virgin

	Matins of the Holy Spirit (begins in the middle . . . *nos autem populus eius* . . .)
fol. 228v	Lauds of the Holy Spirit
fol. 233r	Matins of the Virgin
fol. 247r	Lauds of the Virgin
fol. 253v	Suffrages
fol. 265r	Prime of the Holy Spirit
fol. 268r	Prime of the Virgin
fol. 273r	Tierce of the Holy Spirit
fol. 276r	Tierce of the Virgin
fol. 280r	Sext of the Holy Spirit
fol. 283r	Sext of the Virgin
fol. 287r	Nones of the Holy Spirit
fol. 289r	Memoria to St. Christopher (added)
fol. 290r	Nones of the Virgin
fol. 294r	Vespers of the Holy Spirit
fol. 297r	Vespers of the Virgin
fol. 303r	Compline of the Holy Spirit
fol. 306r	Compline of the Virgin
fol. 311r	Hours of the Cross
	Matins
fol. 315r	Lauds
fol. 320r	Prime
fol. 324r	Tierce
fol. 328r	Sext
fol. 333r	Nones
fol. 338r	Vespers
fol. 342r	Compline
fol. 344r	Memoria to St. Claudius (added)
fol. 346r	Seven Penitential Psalms
fol. 355r	Office of the Dead
fol. 388r	Psalter of St. Jerome
fol. 400r	Office of St. Michael (added)

Calendar

(Abbreviations are expanded. Solar and lunar notations are omitted.)

JANUARY

1. Circumcisio Domini (blue)
2.
3. Genovefe [sic] virginis
4.
5.
6. Epiphania Domini (blue)
7.
8. Sanctorum Luciani Maxiani Juliani martirum
9. Natalis sanctorum Juliani Basillisse martirum
10.
11.
12.
13. Sanctorum Hylarii et Remigii
14. Firmini
15.

16.
17. Sulplicii episcopi
18. Sancte Prisce virginis martiris
19.
20.
21. Agnetis virginis
22. Vincentii martiris
23.
24.
25. Conversio sancti Pauli. Prejecti martiris
26.
27.
28. Sancte Agnetis
29. Valerii episcopi
30.
31.

FEBRUARY

1.
2. Purificatio sancte Marie (blue)
3. Blasii martiris
4.
5. Agathe virginis
6. Vedasti et Amandi episcoporum
7.
8.
9. Octava purificationem
10.
11. Severini abbatis
12.
13.
14.

15.
16. Sancte Juliane virginis et martiris
17.
18.
19.
20.
21.
22. Cathedra santi Petri (red)
23.
24. Mathie apostoli (blue)
25.
26.
27.
28. Romani abbatis

MARCH

1. Sancti Albini episcopi et confessoris
2.

3.
4.

5.
6.
7. Perpetue et Felicitatis
8.
9.
10.
11.
12. Gregorii pape
13.
14. Leonis pape
15.
16.
17.
18.

19.
20.
21. Sancti Benedicti
22.
23.
24.
25. Adnunciatio Dominica (red)
26.
27.
28.
29.
30.
31.

APRIL

1. Sancti Walarici abbatis confessoris
2.
3.
4. Ambrosii episcopi
5.
6.
7.
8.
9.
10.
11. Leonis pape
12.
13. Euphemie virginis
14.
15.

16.
17.
18.
19. Leonis pape
20.
21.
22.
23. Sancti Georgii martiris
24.
25. Marci evangeliste
26. Richarii abbatis
27. Anastasii pape et martiris
28. Vitalis martiris
29.
30.

MAY

1. Philippi et Jacobi
2. Germani episcopi et martiris
3. Inventio sancte Crucis et Alexandri (red)
4. Quiriaci episcopi et martiris
5. Ascensio Domini (blue)
6. Johannis apostoli
7.
8.
9. Translatio sancti Nicholai episcopi et confessoris
10.
11.

12.
13.
14.
15.
16. Honorati episcopi et confessoris (blue)
17.
18.
19.
20.
21.
22.
23. Desiderii episcopi et confessoris

24.
25.
26. Augustini episcopi et confessoris
27.

28. Germani episcopi et confessoris
29. Maximi episcopi et confessoris
30.
31. Petronille virginis

JUNE

1. Nichomedis martiris
2. Marcellini et Petri martiris
3.
4.
5.
6.
7.
8. Medardi et Gildardi episcoporum
   confessorum
9. Primi et Feliciani martirum
10.
11. Barnabe apostoli
12.
13.
14. Rufini et Valerii martirum
15.
16.

17.
18. Marci et Marcelliani martirum
19. Gervasii et Prothasii martirum (red)
20.
21.
22.
23. Vigilia. Missa (red)
24. Nativitas sancti Johannis Baptista
    (blue)
25. Translatio sancti Eligii episcopi et
    confessoris
26. Johannis et Pauli martirum
27.
28. Vigilia apostolorum. Missa (red)
29. Petri et Pauli apostolorum (blue)
30. Commemoratio sancti Pauli (red)

JULY

1. Octava sancti Johannis Baptista (red)
2. Processi et Marciniani martirum
3.
4. Translatio sancti Martini (red)
5.
6. Octava apostolorum (red)
7.
8.
9.
10. Septem fratrem martires
11. Translatio sancti Benedicti abbatis
12.
13.
14.
15. Relatio sancti Vedasti episcopi et
    confessoris
16.
17.

18. Arnulphi episcopi et martiris
19.
20. Margarete virginis et martiris
21. Victoris martiris. Praxedis virginis
    et martiris
22. Marie Magdalene (blue)
23.
24.
25. Jacobi apostoli (blue)
26.
27.
28.
29. Felicis, Simplicii, Faustini et
    Beatricis martirum
30.
31. Germani episcopi et confessoris
    antisodorum

AUGUST

1. Petri ad vincula (red)
2.
3. Inventio sancti Stephani martiris
4.
5.
6. Sexti pape et martiris
7. Donati episcopi et martiris
8.
9. Romani martiris. Vigilia (red).
   Missa (red)
10. Laurentii martiris (red)
11.
12.
13. Ypoliti martiris sociorumque eius
14. Vigilia (red)
15. Assumptio beate Marie virginis (blue)
16. Arnulphi episcopi et confessoris

17. Octava sancti Laurentii
18. Agapiti martiris
19.
20.
21.
22. Octava beate Marie
23. Vigilia (red)
24. Bartholomei apostoli (red)
25.
26.
27. Rufi martiris
28. Augustini episcopi et confessoris
29. Decollatio sancti Johannis Baptista
    (blue)
30.
31. Paulini episcopi et confessoris

SEPTEMBER

1. Firmini episcopi et confessoris (blue)
2. Arnulphi martiris
3.
4. Marcellis martiris
5.
6.
7.
8. Nativitas beate Marie (red)
9.
10.
11. Prothi et Jacincti martirum
12.
13.
14. Exaltatio sancte Crucis (red)
15. Octava beate Marie
16.

17. Lamberti episcopi et martiris
18.
19.
20. Vigilia. Missa (red)
21. Mathei apostoli et evangeliste (blue)
22. Mauricii sociorumque eius et
    martirum
23.
24.
25. Firmini episcopi et martiris (blue)
26.
27. Cosme et Damiani martirum
28.
29. Michaelis archangeli (blue)
30. Jeronimi presbiteris et confessoris

OCTOBER

1. Vedasti episcopi et confessoris.
   Remigii et aliorum (red)
2. Octava sancti Firmini
3. Dionisii episcopi et martiris
4.
5.
6.

7. Marci pape et confessoris
8. Benedicte virginis
9. Dyonisii, Rustici et Eructerii [sic]
   martirum
10.
11.
12.

13.
14.
15.
16. Octava sancti Dyonisii
17.
18. Luce evangeliste
19.
20.
21.
22.

23.
24.
25. Crispini et Crispiniani martirum
26. Amandi episcopi et confessoris
27. Vigilia. Missa (red)
28. Symonis et Jude apostolorum (blue)
29.
30.
31. Quintini martiris. Vigilia omnium
    sanctorum (red)

NOVEMBER

1. Oomnium [sic] sanctorum (blue)
2. Commemoratio fidelium defunc-
   torum (red)
3.
4.
5.
6.
7.
8.
9. Theodori martiris
10. Martini pape et confessoris
11. Transitus sancti Martini (red)
12.
13.
14.
15.

16. Eutherii episcopi et confessoris
17.
18. Octava sancti Martini
19. Gregorii episcopi et confessoris
20.
21.
22. Cecilie virginis et martiris
23. Clementis pape et martiris
24.
25. Katherine virginis et martiris
26. Lini pape et martiris
27.
28.
29. Saturnini martiris. Vigilia (blue).
    Missa (blue)
30. Sancti Andree apostoli (blue)

DECEMBER

1. Constantiani abbatis
2.
3.
4.
5.
6. Nicholai episcopi et confessoris (red)
7. Octava sancti Andree
8. Conceptio beate Marie (blue)
9.
10.
11. Fuciani, Victorici et Genciani (red)
12. Vualarici abbatis
13. Lucie virginis. Octava sancti Nicholai
14. Nichasii sociorumque eius (red)
15.
16.

17.
18.
19.
20.
21. Thome apostoli (red)
22.
23.
24. Vigilia natalis Domini (red)
25. Natalis Domini (blue)
26. Stephani prothomartiris (blue)
27. Johannis evangeliste (blue)
28. Sanctorum Innocentum (blue)
29. Thome archiepiscopi et martiris
    (blue)
30.
31. Silvestri pape et confessoris (red)

Litany

fol. 196r Sancta Trinitas unus Deus
Spiritus sancte Deus
Sancta Maria
Sancta Dei genitrix
Sancta Virgo virginum
Sancte Michael
Sancte Gabriel
fol. 196v Sancte Raphael
Omnes sancti angeli et
archangeli
Sancte Iohannes Baptista
Omnes sancti patriarche et
prophete
Sancte Petre
Sancte Paule
Sancte Andrea
Sancte Iacobe
Sancte Iohannes
Sancte Thoma
Sancte Iacobe
Sancte Philippe
Sancte Bartholomee
Sancte Mathee
Sancte Simon
Sancte Thadee
Sancte Mathia
Sancte Barnaba
Sancte Marce
fol. 197r Sancte Luca
Omnes sancti apostoli et
evangeliste
Omnes sancti discipuli
Domini
Omnes sancti innocentes
Sancte Stephane
Sancte Line
Sancte Clete
Sancte Clemens
Sancte Syrce
Sancte Laurenti
Sancte Vincenti
Sancte Gorgoni
Sancte Blasi
Sancte Pataleon [sic]

Sancte Dyonisi cum sociis
tuis
Sancte Maurici cum sociis
tuis
Sancte Nereo cum sociis
tuis
Sancte Victor cum sociis
tuis
Sancte Cosma
fol. 197v Sancte Damiane
Sancte Fabiane
Sancte Sebastiane
Sancte Thiburci
Sancte Agapite
Sancte Georgi
Sancte Lamberte
Sancte Christofore
Sancte Seessari [sic]
Sancte Maure
Omnes sancti martyres
Sancte Silvester
Sancte Gregori
Sancte Leo
Sancte Hylari
Sancte Martine
Sancte Severine
Sancte Servaci
Sancte Ambrosi
fol. 198r Sancte Augustine
Sancte Nicholae
Sancte Jeromnime [sic]
Sancte Remigi
Sancte Germane
Sancte Arnulphe
Sancte Benedicte
Sancte Maure
Sancte Paule
Sancte Antoni
Sancte Egidi
Sancte Columbane
Sancte Magne
Sancte Symeon
Sancte Kuniberte
Omnes sancti confessores

Sancta Felicitas
Sancta Perpetua
Sancta Petronilla
fol. 198v Sancta Agatha
Sancta Anna
Sancta Agnes
Sancta Cecilia
Sancta Lucia
Sancta Candida
Sancta Barbara
Sancta Katherina
Sancta Margareta
Sancta Eugenia
Sancta Thecla

Sancta Anastasia
Sancta Columba
Sancta Scolastica
Sancta Fides
Sancta Karitas
Sancta Gertrudis
Sancta Orotildis
Sancta Affra
fol. 199r Sancta Maria Magdalene
Sancta Maria Egyptiaca
Sancta Uundena [sic]
    virginum milia
Sancte Vidue et continentes
Omnes sancti et sancte Dei

Suffrages

fol. 253v	De Trinitate	fol. 258v	De sancto Nicholao
fol. 254r	De Sancto Spiritu		De sancto Eligio
	De Cruce	fol. 259r	De confessoribus
fol. 254v	De angelis		De sancta Maria Magdalene
fol. 255r	De sancto Johanne Baptista	fol. 259v	De sancta Agnetis
fol. 255v	De sancta Maria	fol. 260r	Sancta Katherine
	De sancto Petro (and Paul)	fol. 260v	(Elizabeth of Hungary)
fol. 256r	De sancto Johanne evangeliste	fol. 261r	Undecim milia virgines
			De virginibus
	De sancto Andrea	fol. 261v	De omnibus sanctis
fol. 256v	De apostolis	fol. 262r	(James the Greater)
	De sancto Stephano	fol. 262v	De sancta Margareta
fol. 257r	De sancto Laurento		Sancte Maure
fol. 257v	De sancto Nichasio	fol. 263v	Decem milia martires (added)
	De martyribus		
fol. 258r	De sancto Martino	fol. 264r	De sancto Antonio (added)

Index of Manuscripts

Amiens, Bibliothèque Municipale
MS 124 (Psalter): 39–43, 45–46, 49–50, 52–54
MS 156 (Missal): 41–43, 48–54, 59
MS 157 (Missal): 36–39, 42–43, 46, 50, 52–53, 59
MS 267 (Raimond de Pennaforte, *Summa*): 43 n.32

Arras, Bibliothèque Municipale
MS 88 (Psalter): 18 n.67
MS 230 [907] (Ordinal): 18 n.67

Bari, San Nicola
Proser: 90 n.67

Berlin, Deutsche Staatsbibliothek
MS Hamilton 363 (Romance of the Maccabees): 54

Bonn, Universitätsbibliothek
MS 526 (Arthurian cycle): 54–56

Cambridge
Corpus Christi College
MS 16 (Matthew Paris, *Chronica Majora*): 86, 92–94
MS 26 (Matthew Paris, *Chronica*): 86 n.53
Fitzwilliam Museum
MS 300 (Isabelle Psalter): 59

Darmstadt, Hessiche Landes- und Hochschulbibliothek
MS 2777: 100

Ghent, Library of the City and the University
MS 244: 109 n.111

Hildesheim, Library of St. Godehard
St. Albans Psalter: 70 n.9

London, British Library
MS Add. 17341 (Evangeliary): 58, 61–63
MS Roy. 2 A. xxii (Psalter): 87 n.53
MS Roy. 2 B. iii: 100 n.90, 103 n.98

Marseille, Bibliothèque Municipale
MS 111 (Book of Hours): 95 n.79

Montpellier, Faculté de Médecine
  MS 360: 108 n.111

New York
  Cloisters Collection
    MS 54.1.2 (Hours of Jeanne d'Evreux): 27 n.7, 113 n.119
  Pierpont Morgan Library
    M60 (Book of Hours): 74 n.20
    M72 (Psalter of Gérard de Damville): 95
    M796 (Psalter): 44–46, 49–50, 52–53

Paris, Bibliothèque Nationale
  MS fr. 95 (*Histoire du Graal . . .*): 55–56
  MS fr. 1159 (*Livre de Sidrach*): 49–51, 53, 62 n.76
  MS fr. 9220 (*Vergier de Solas*): 101, 103 n.98
  MS lat. 1023 (Breviary of Philippe le Bel): 60
  MS lat. 10435 (Psalter): 46–49, 51–54
  MS lat. 10525 (Psalter of St. Louis): 27, 59
  MS lat. 12834 (Martyrology of Saint-Germain-des-Prés): 57–58, 61,
    62 n.75, 63
  MS n.a. lat. 3093 (*Très Belles Heures de Notre-Dame*): 113 n.119,
    n.120

Princeton, University Library
  Garrett MS 125 (Gautier de Belleperche, *Le Roman de Judas Machabée*;
    Chrétien de Troyes, *Yvain*): 54

Private collection, Comte du Boisrouvray
  Psalter: 54, 105, 107

The Hague
  Bibliothèque Royale
    MS 78 D 40 (Missal): 52 n.49
  Mus. Meermanno-Westreenianum
    MS 10 B 23 (Bible of Jean de Vaudetar): 27 n.7

Troyes, Bibliothèque Municipale
  MS 106 (Bible): 10 n.40

Turin, Biblioteca Nazionale
  MS E. V. 49 (*Heures de Savoie*, now destroyed, fragments at Yale University, Beinecke Library, MS 390): 113 n.119

Vatican City
  MS Vat. lat. 1058: 100 n.90, 103 n.98

ILLUSTRATIONS

Yolande of Soissons with Her Family, *fol. 1v*

*Figures 1–39 are from the Psalter and Hours of Yolande of Soissons, New York,
Pierpont Morgan Library, M729 (photos: Pierpont Morgan Library).*

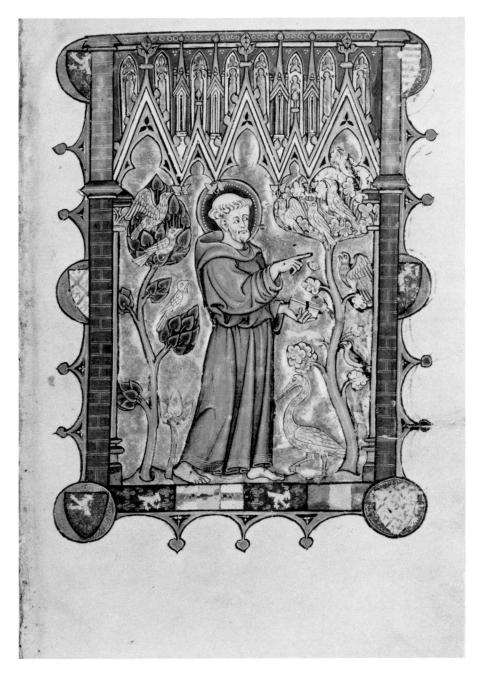

St. Francis Preaching to the Birds, *fol. 2r*

The Invention of the Body of St. Firmin, *fol. 3r*

Crucifixion, *fol. 4v*

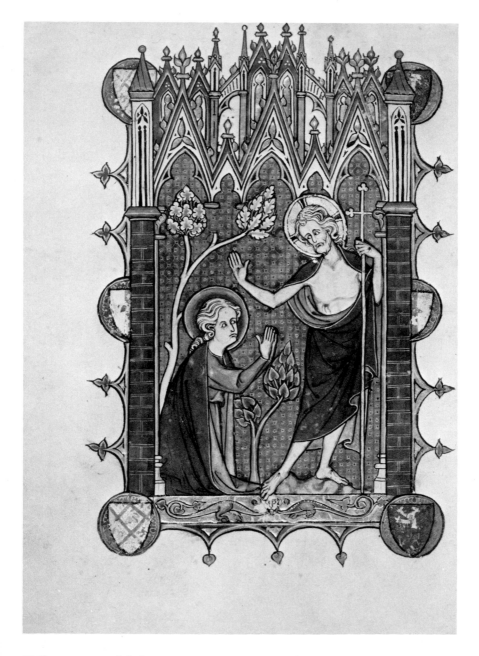

Noli me tangere, *fol. 6v*

Iunius in darno quindeni a fine
ꝗ salutem.

Nichomelis mris.
Marcellini er petri mris.

rur | f | iiij | ꝗꝓ
viij | g | iii |
rvi | b | ii |
v | b | c | Nonas
| c | vur | iᵭ
rıııı | d | vuj | iᵭ
ıı | e | vij | iᵭ Medardı er gildardı eꝓum conf.
| f | vı | iᵭ Primi er feliciani mıɽ.
r | g | v | iᵭ
| a | iiij | iᵭ Barnabe apłi.
rvıı | b | ii | iᵭ
vıj | c | d | Idus
| d | rvıı | kł ufini ꝛ ualerii
rv | e | rvj | kł mıɽ.
iıı | f | rvı | kł
| g | rv | kł ſol ıntrauit
rıı | a | rııı | kł Marcı er marcelliani mıɽ.
ı | b | rııı | kł Gervasıı ꝛ prothasıı mr̄.
| c | rıı | kł Solſtanıı.
ır | d | rı | kł
| e | r | kł
rvıı | f | ır | kł Uıgılıa Iılla.
vı | g | dovıı | kł Nat s ıohannıs baptıſte.
| a | vuj | kł Tranſlacıo s eligii epı er conf.
rııı | b | vıı | kł Iohannıs er paulı mıɽ.
uıj | c | vı | kł
| d | v | kł Uıgılıa apłorum Mıſſa
rı | e | iiij | kł Petrı er paulı apłorum.
| f | ii | kł Commemoracıo s paulı

6

Calendar: July, *fol. 11r*

Holy Face, *fol. 15r*

Beatus Page, *fol. 16r*

Psalm 26: David Looking to God, *fol. 40r*

Temptation on the Mountain, *fol. 55v*

Adducentur regi urgines post eam: p
rime eius afferentur tibi.
Afferentur in leticia et exultatione: ad
ducentur in templum regis.
Pro patribz tuis nati sunt tibi filij: consti
tues eos principes sup omnem tram.
Memores erunt nominis tui domine: i
omni generatione et generationem.
Propterea ipli confitebuntur tibi in eter
num: et in seculum seculi.
Deus nr refugium et uirtus: adiutor
in tribulationibz que inuenerunt
nos nimis.
Propterea n timebimus dum turbabit
tra: transferentur montes in cor maris.
Sonuerunt et turbate sunt aque eor: co
turbati sunt montes i fortitudine eius
Fluminis impetus letificat ciuitate dei
sctificauit tabernaclm suum altissimus.

Text: Psalter, *fol. 63v*

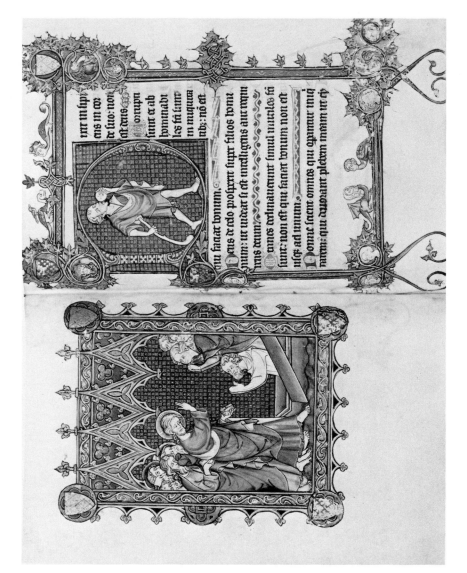

Raising of Lazarus, *fol. 70v*

Psalm 52: The Fool, *fol. 71r*

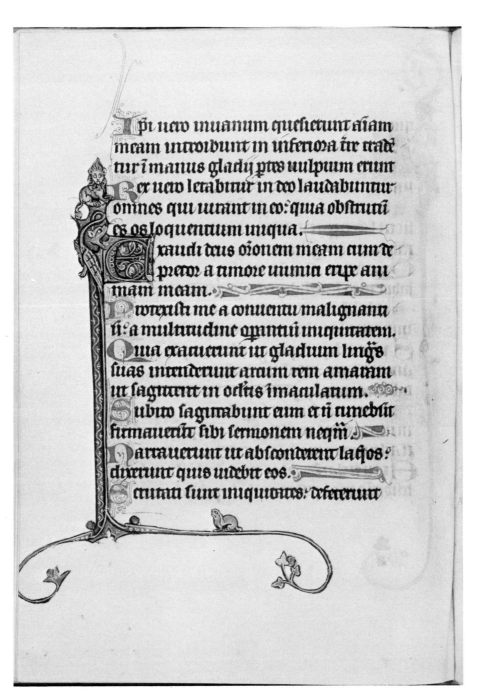

Text: Psalter, *fol. 79v*

Miracle of the Loaves, *fol. 85v*

Healing the Blind Man at the Pool of Siloam, *fol. 104v*

Woman Taken in Adultery, *fol. 122v*

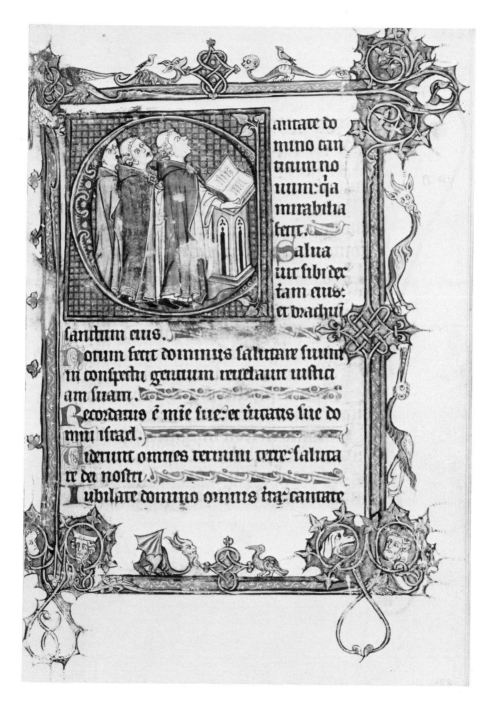

antate do
mino can
ticum no
uum:qa
mirabilia
fent.

Salua
uit fibi dex
tam cius:
et brachui

sanctum cius.

Notum fecit dominus salutare suum:
in conspectu gentium reuelauit iusticti
am suam.

Recordatus e mie sue: et iuitatis sue do
mui israel.

Uiderunt omnes termini terre:saluta
re dei nostri.

Iubilate domino omnis tra:cantate

Psalm 97: Priests Singing, *fol. 123r*

Litany: Priests Singing, *fol. 196r*

Yolande of Soissons Praying, *fol. 232v*

Matins of the Virgin: Annunciation, *fol. 233r*

Nativity, *fol. 246v*

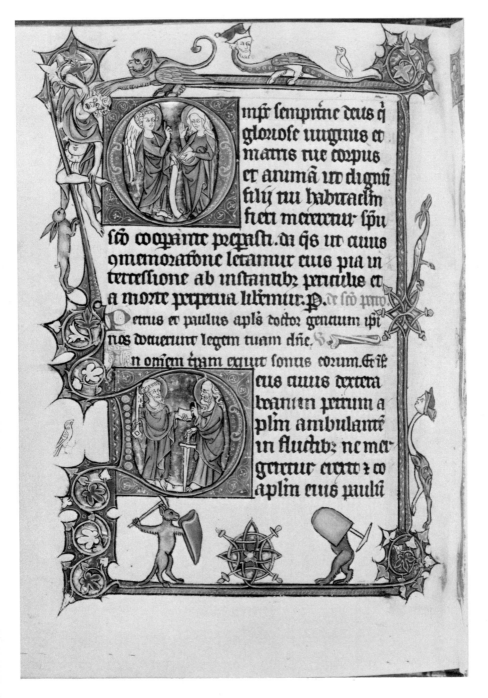

Suffrages: Annunciation and Saints Peter and Paul, *fol. 255v*

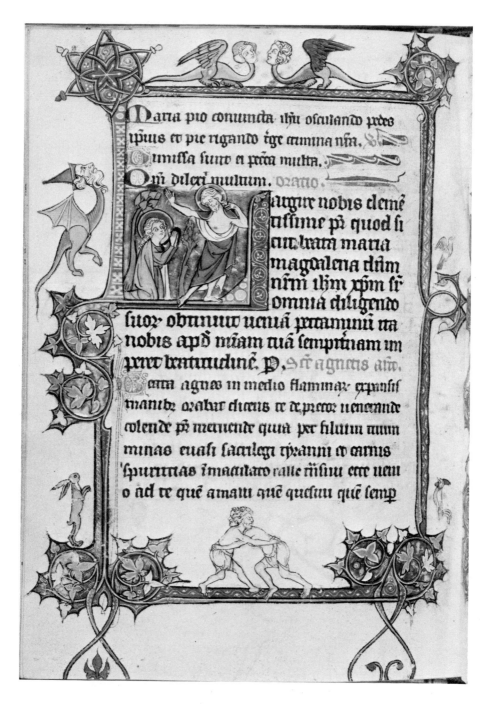

Suffrages: Noli me tangere, *fol. 259v*

24

Prime of the Virgin: Magi before Herod, *fol. 268r*

Creation of the Plants, *fol. 272v*

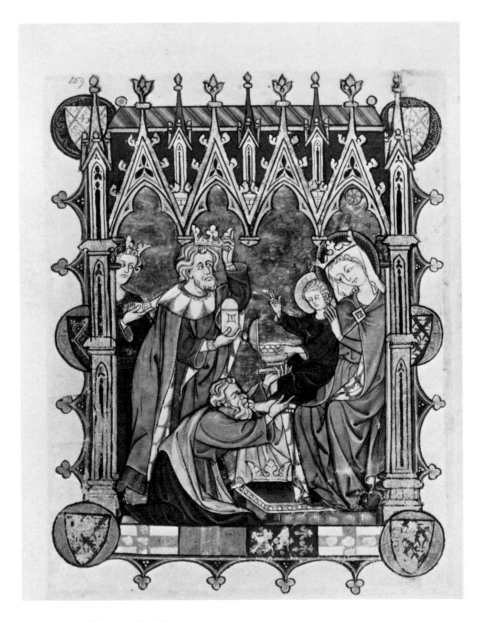

Adoration of the Magi, *fol. 275v*

Nones of the Holy Spirit: Peter Healing a Lame Man, *fol. 287r*

Legend of the Cornfield, *fol. 289v*

Massacre of the Innocents, *fol. 296v*

Death of the Virgin, *fol. 305v*

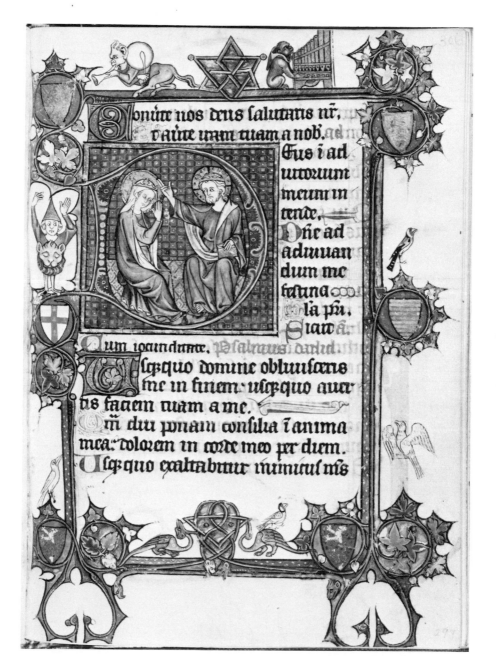

Compline of the Virgin: Coronation of the Virgin, *fol. 306r*

Text: Hours of the Virgin, *fol. 309r*

Entry into Jerusalem, *fol. 310v*

34

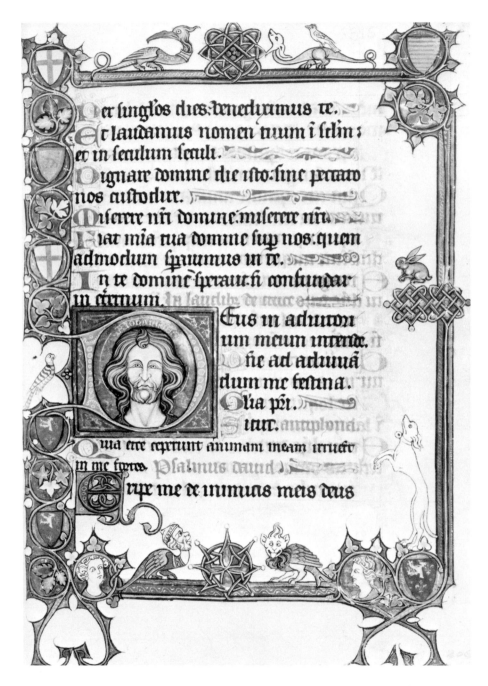

Lauds of the Cross: St. John, *fol. 315r*

Crucifixion, *fol. 332v*

Crucifixion, *fol. 337v*

Tree of Life, *fol. 345v*

Unicorn Parable, *fol. 354v*

In vigilia mortuorum. antiphona.

Placebo domino. Ps. dilexi quoniam exaudiet dominus uocem orationis mee. Quia inclinauit aurem suam michi: et in diebus meis inuocabo. Circundederunt me dolores mortis: et pericula inferni inuenerunt me. Tribulacionem et dolorem inueni: et nomen domini inuocaui. O domine libera aiam meam: misericors diis et iustus: et deus noster miseretur.

Office of the Dead: Funeral Rites, *fol. 355r*

Amiens Cathedral, Chevet
  (photo: James Austin)

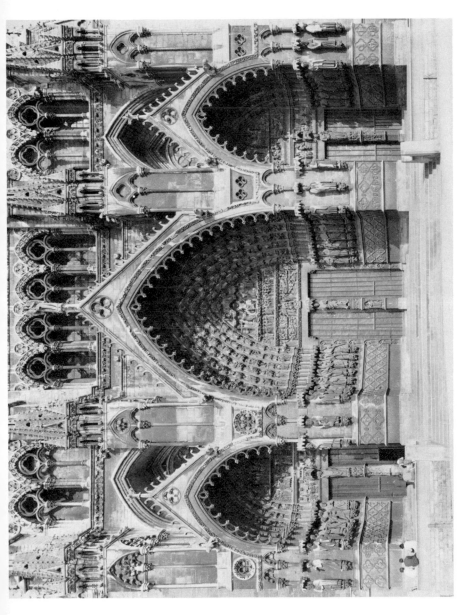

Amiens Cathedral, West Façade
(photo: James Austin)

Psalter of St. Louis: Balaam and His Ass
Paris, Bibliothèque Nationale, MS lat. 10525, fol. 39v
 (photo: Bibliothèque Nationale)

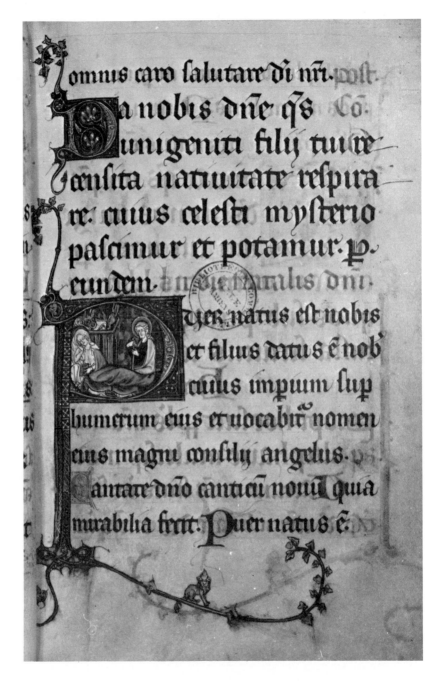

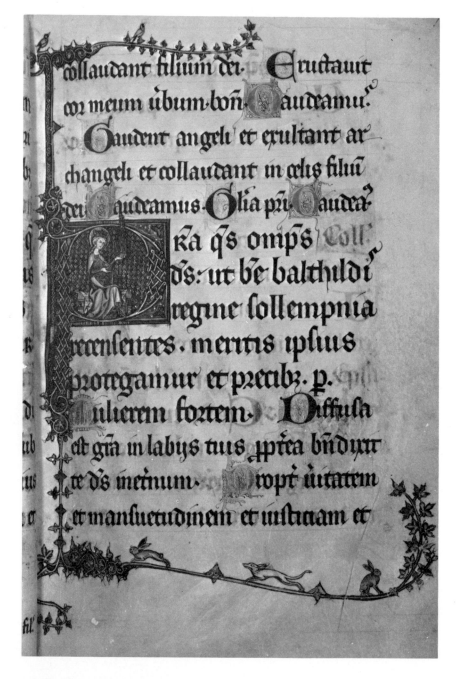

Missal: Queen Bathildis

Amiens, Bibliothèque Municipale, MS 157, fol. 29r

(photo: Bibliothèque Municipale, Amiens)

Missal: Crucifixion
Amiens, Bibliothèque Municipale, MS 157, fol. 109v
(photo: Bibliothèque Municipale, Amiens)

Missal: Coronation of the Virgin
Amiens, Bibliothèque Municipale, MS 157, fol. 110r
(photo: Bibliothèque Municipale, Amiens)

47. Psalter: Calendar, November
Amiens, Bibliothèque Municipale, MS 124, fol. 6r
(photo: Bibliothèque Municipale, Amiens)

48. Psalter: Beatus Page
Amiens, Bibliothèque Municipale, MS 124, fol. 17v
(photo: Bibliothèque Municipale, Amiens)

49. Missal: Nativity
Amiens, Bibliothèque Municipale,
  MS 156, fol. 21r
  (photo: Bibliothèque Municipale, Amiens)

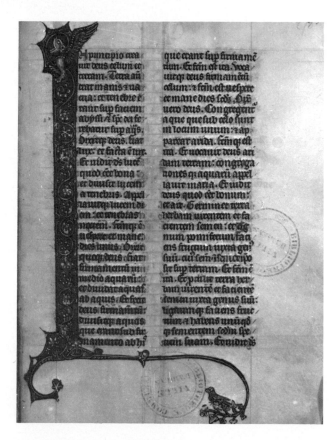

50. Missal: Decorated Initial
Amiens, Bibliothèque Municipale, MS 156, fol. 273r
  (photo: Bibliothèque Municipale, Amiens)

Psalter: Beatus Page
New York, Pierpont Morgan Library, M796, fol. 1r
(photo: Pierpont Morgan Library)

52

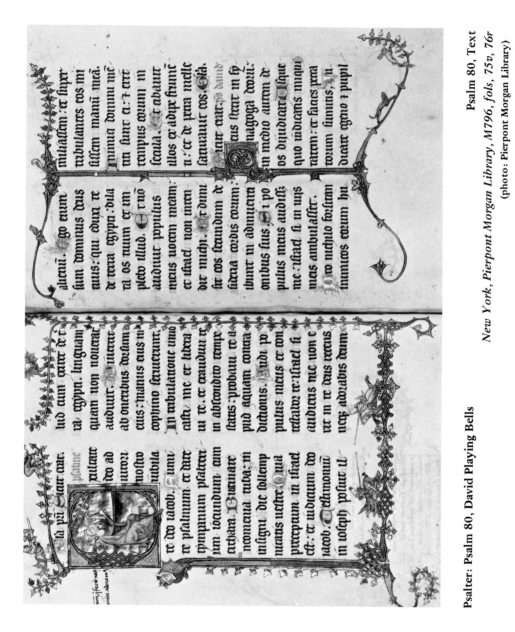

Psalter: Psalm 80, David Playing Bells

Psalm 80, Text

New York, Pierpont Morgan Library, M796, fols, 75v, 76r

(photo: Pierpont Morgan Library)

Psalter: Psalm 109, God and Christ
Pierpont Morgan Library, M796, fol. 106r

(photo: Pierpont Morgan Library)

54

Psalter: Beatus Page
Paris, Bibliothèque Nationale, MS lat. 10435, fol. 1r
(photo: Bibliothèque Nationale)

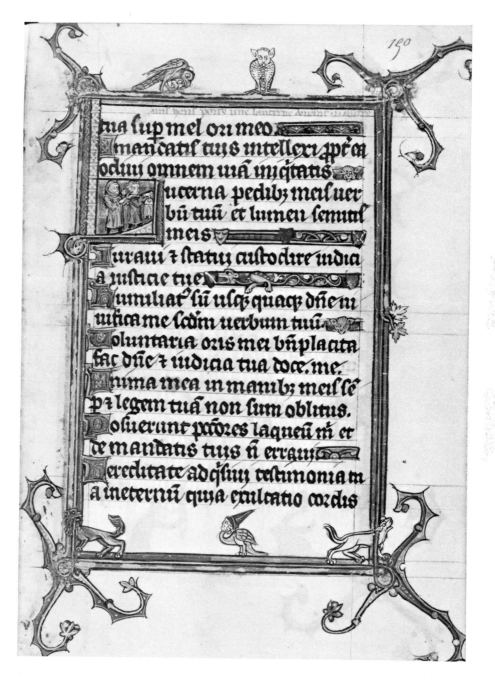

Psalter: Psalm 119
Paris, Bibliothèque Nationale, MS lat. 10435, fol. 150r
(photo: Bibliothèque Nationale)

Livre de Sidrach: Noah Directing the Animals to the Ark
Paris, *Bibliothèque Nationale, MS fr. 1159, fol. 59v*
(photo: Bibliothèque Nationale)

Arthurian Cycle

Bonn, Universitätsbibliothek, MS 526, fol. 1r
(photo: Universitätsbibliothek, Bonn)

Histoire du Graal
Paris, Bibliothèque Nationale, MS fr. 95, fol. 1r
  (photo: Bibliothèque Nationale)

Histoire du Graal
Paris, Bibliothèque Nationale, MS fr. 95, fol. 205r
(photo: Bibliothèque Nationale)

60. Martyrology of Saint-Germain-des-Prés: July
Paris, Bibliothèque Nationale, MS lat. 12834, fol. 59v
(photo: Bibliothèque Nationale)

61. Evangeliary: Entry into Jerusalem
London, British Library, MS Add. 17341, fol. 1r
(photo: British Library)

Evangeliary: Genesis Initial
London, British Library, MS Add. 17341, fol. 11r
(photo: British Library)

Tomb of Adelaide of Champagne
Joigny, Saint-Jean
(photo: Hirmer Fotoarchiv München)

Matthew Paris, *Chronica Majora:* Veronica
Cambridge, Corpus Christi College, MS 16, fol. 49v
(photo: Courtauld Institute)

The Holy Face
Laon Cathedral

Psalter of Gérard de Damville: St. Francis Preaching to the Birds
New York, Pierpont Morgan Library, M72, fol. 139v
(photo: Pierpont Morgan Library)

67

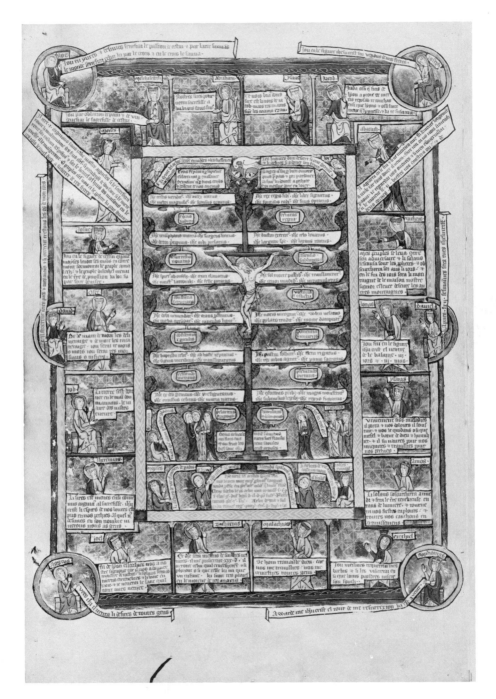

Vergier de Solas: **Tree of Life**
Paris, Bibliothèque Nationale, MS fr. 9220, fol. 9v
(photo: Bibliothèque Nationale)

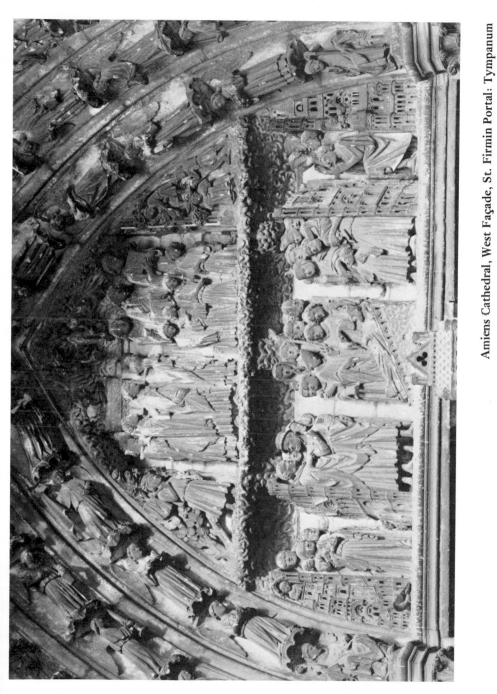

Amiens Cathedral, West Façade, St. Firmin Portal: Tympanum
(photo: James Austin)